CIVIL WAR A〜Z

OTHER CIVIL WAR TITLES FROM
RANDOM HOUSE VALUE PUBLISHING

CIVIL WAR
A ～ Z

MARSHA E. KALMAN

GRAMERCY BOOKS
New York

This book is dedicated to my father-in-law, James Barnette

Hicks, whose fascination with American history is contagious, and

to my husband, David, and my daughter, Shira, whose love and

support are the joy of my life.

This 2000 edition is published by Gramercy Books™, an imprint of Random House Value Publishing, Inc. 280 Park Avenue, New York, N.Y. 10017.

Gramercy Books™ and design are trademarks of Random House Value Publishing, Inc.

Random House
New York • Toronto • London • Sydney • Auckland
http://www.randomhouse.com/

Printed and bound in the United States of America.

Text Design by Karen Ocker Design

Library of Congress Cataloging-in-Publication Data

Kalman, Marsha E.
    The Civil War A to Z / Marsha E. Kalman.
        p. cm.
    ISBN 0-517-16211-3
        1. United States–History–Civil War, 1861-1865–Dictionaries. I. Title.

E468 .K2 2000
973.7'03–dc21

00-024504

INTRODUCTION

The Civil War was a turning point in the history of the United States. Almost 620,000 Americans died during the war, nearly as many as died in all the wars from the Revolution through Vietnam combined. The nature of warfare was changed forever. Submarines and ironclad ships, observation balloons, railroads, telegraphs, and land mines were used in war for the first time, and new military strategies and weapons were introduced. The Southern way of life was destroyed, and the newly unified nation emerged as a major world power.

The legacy of the Civil War remains very much a part of American culture. Even as this book was going to press, it was hard to open a newspaper or turn on the radio without coming across stories that had their genesis during the Civil War. Heated disputes rage over whether the Confederate flag should be flown at the capitol building in South Carolina. A controversial observation tower on the Gettysburg battlefield is razed. Women in the military and African-Americans throughout the nation continue their on-going struggles for equal rights.

Countless books have been written about the Civil War, and this one does not pretend to be definitive. Rather, through its nearly 200 alphabetical entries, *Civil War A-Z* provides a point of reference for the general reader. It describes the important, and sometimes unusual, people, ideas, and events of the war. *Civil War A-Z* covers all of the basics–military battles and campaigns from Fort Sumter to Appomattox Court House, the principal generals and politicians, and the social and historical background of the war and its aftermath, from the growth of the abolition movement to Reconstruction. It offers a glimpse at some of the technological innovations that played a role in the war, from the early use of submarines and aeronautical reconnaissance to Mathew Brady's photographic documentation of the war. *Civil War A-Z* also includes biographical sketches of people whose contributions often have been overlooked in standard accounts of the war. In these pages you'll read about audacious women like Elizabeth Van Lew and Loreta Janeta Velazquez, who served in the war as spies and soldiers, about Robert Smalls, a slave who brazenly piloted a Confederate supply boat to freedom, and about Ely Samuel Parker, the highest-ranking Native American officer in the Union army, and his Confederate counterpart, Stand Watie. My hope is that these brief introductions to the fascinating people and events of the Civil War will bring the era to life for you and perhaps inspire you to seek out further information.

Marsha E. Kalman

July 2000

ABOLITIONIST MOVEMENT

Regional opposition to slavery in the colonies began almost as early as 1624, resulting in the abolition of slavery in much of the North before the Revolutionary War. An organized national antislavery movement began with the formation in December 1833 of the first national abolitionist group, the American Anti-Slavery Society. This organization advocated both the immediate end of slavery and full political rights for blacks; it opposed reforms proposed by less militant abolitionists, such as the curtailment of the expansion of slavery, the financial compensation of ex-slaveholders, and the colonization movement, which in 1822 had started settling emancipated slaves in what is now the African country of Liberia.

Passage of the Fugitive Slave Act in 1850 and the publication in 1852 of *Uncle Tom's Cabin* brought new support to the movement. Abolitionists—men and women, black and white—were responsible for the Underground Railroad that led many fugitive slaves to freedom. Noted abolitionists included William Lloyd Garrison, editor of *The Liberator* and one of the founders of the Anti-Slavery Society; African-American author and orator Frederick Douglass; orator and former slave Sojourner Truth; and Angelina and Sarah Grimké, lecturers and co-authors of *American Slavery As It Is*, the second-most influential antislavery book of the era.

With the ratification of the Thirteenth Amendment in 1865, slavery was officially abolished in the United States. The Anti-Slavery Society was disbanded in 1870, but many abolitionists continued to work throughout Reconstruction to ensure the political, educational, and economic rights of the emancipated slaves.

AFRICAN-AMERICAN SOLDIERS

The South never officially used African Americans in combat, although slaves worked as servants and

laborers for the army. On March 14, 1865, a desperate Confederate Congress authorized the enlistment of black soldiers, but the war ended before recruitment got started.

Almost 180,000 African-Americans served in the Union army, and approximately 37,300 died in action. Until the Emancipation Proclamation of 1863, however, blacks were classified as "contraband," in the same category as other Confederate property seized by the Union; they were used as laborers but were not permitted to carry weapons. After the Emancipation Proclamation, African-American soldiers fought in segregated units under the command of white officers, such as the 54th Massachusetts Regiment, which was commanded by Colonel Robert Gould Shaw. Black troops did not receive the same pay and clothing allowances as white soldiers until June 1864. Fewer than 100 blacks became Union officers, and none advanced beyond the rank of captain.

ANACONDA PLAN

In 1861, Union General-in-Chief Winfield Scott conceived a strategy that would defeat the South while limiting bloodshed, by controlling the Mississippi River with troops and gunboats and blockading Southern ports. Viewed as too cautious by critics who thought that the war would be over in six weeks, Scott's Anaconda Plan effectively weakened the Confederacy and, along with the battles he had hoped to avoid, brought about the Union victory.

ROBERT ANDERSON
(1805-1871)

Robert Anderson was the commander of Fort Sumter whose surrender to the Confederates on April 14, 1861, marked the beginning of the Civil War. Promoted to brigadier general by Lincoln on May 15, 1861, in recognition of his service at Fort Sumter, Anderson went on to command the Department of Kentucky and the Department of the Cumberland. Although he retired in 1863, he returned to raise the Union flag at Fort Sumter following its recapture in 1865.

ANDERSONVILLE PRISON
(FEBRUARY 1864-APRIL 1865)

The most notorious of the Civil War military prisons, Andersonville, officially known as Camp Sumter, was built in southwestern Georgia to handle the overflow of Northern prisoners-of-war who had been held near Richmond. By July 1864, over 32,000 soldiers were held in the open-air facility, which was originally intended to hold 10,000 prisoners. A stagnant stream that flowed through the middle of the camp was used for drinking, bathing, and sewage. Some prisoners defied regulations and erected flimsy shelters, but most were fully exposed to the elements because there were no barracks. Starvation was rampant, and virtually no medical care was available.

By the end of the war, over 45,000 Union soldiers had been imprisoned at Andersonville, more than at any other Confederate prison. Official records indicate that at least 12,912 soldiers died there. Extreme shortages of supplies and poor management rather than deliberate cruelty may have been responsible

for much of the horror of Andersonville Prison; indeed, conditions were not much better for Confederate prisoners-of-war held in Union facilities, including one in Elmira, New York, that had a death rate nearly as great as Andersonville's. Nevertheless, Andersonville's commander, Captain Henry Wirz, was convicted of war crimes and was hanged on November 10, 1865, the only person to be executed as a result of the Civil War.

ANDREWS' RAID
(APRIL 12, 1862)

Twenty-one soldiers from Ohio, led by Union spy John J. Andrews, sabotaged a critical link in the supply chain between Atlanta and Chattanooga, on April 12, 1862. The raiders, disguised as civilians, boarded a northbound train in Marietta, Georgia, and, during the breakfast stop, detached the passenger cars and rode off in *The General*, the train's locomotive. As they headed for Tennessee, they cut telegraph wires, burned or blocked tracks, and destroyed bridges and tunnels. Pursued by the train's conductor on foot, by handcar, and then in the locomotive *Texas*, "The Great Locomotive Chase" lasted for only 90 miles before *The General* ran out of fuel. The raiders fled into the woods, but all of them were captured and imprisoned by the Confederates. Andrews and seven others were executed as spies in Atlanta; eight of the others escaped in October 1862. The remaining six prisoners were released a year later and became the first soldiers to receive the Medal of Honor.

ANTIETAM (SHARPSBURG), CAMPAIGN AND BATTLE OF (SEPTEMBER 17, 1862)

The Battle of Antietam, fought on September 17, 1862, marked the bloodiest day of a blood-drenched war. More than 27,000 men died in the twelve-hour battle.

Seeking to capture the federal rail center at Harrisburg, Pennsylvania, General Robert E. Lee divided the Army of Northern Virginia into three groups. He sent nearly half of the army with General Thomas J. "Stonewall" Jackson to capture the Union fort at Harpers Ferry, Virginia, after which they were to combine forces with General James Longstreet's divisions and march together to rejoin the remainder of Lee's troops near Harrisburg. Fate intervened, however, on September 13, when a Union corporal discovered a copy of Lee's strategy wrapped around three cigars near an abandoned Confederate camp. Fearing that the document was a Confederate ploy, Union General George McClellan did not take immediate action.

When the fighting did get started, heavy Confederate losses led Lee to prepare to retreat to Virginia, until he learned of Jackson's September 15 victory at Harpers Ferry. Bolstered by the win, and by the much-needed supplies obtained from the captured garrison, Lee ordered all of his troops to Sharpsburg, a town on the Antietam Creek in Maryland. McClellan held off again, until 6:00 AM on September 17, when 75,000 Union soldiers faced off against 40,000 Confederate troops. Only the arrival of General A.P. Hill's division from Harpers Ferry saved the Confederate army from what might have been complete destruction. Lee's army retreated to Virginia the following evening.

Antietam was viewed as an important victory for the North, and a major turning point in the war. Bolstered by the Union victory, Lincoln issued his preliminary Emancipation Proclamation five days later, on September 22, effectively shifting the focus of the war from maintaining the Union to ending slavery—and opening up the Union army to black recruits. Antietam also represented the end of McClellan's military career. His cautious nature and his failure to pursue and crush Lee's retreating army led Lincoln to remove McClellan from command in November 1862.

APPOMATTOX COURT HOUSE
(APRIL 9, 1865)

On April 8, 1865, General George Custer captured Confederate supply trains near this Virginia town located nine miles west of Richmond and 180 miles south of Washington, D.C., as several Union divisions surrounded General Robert E. Lee's forces, blocking their escape route to Lynchburg. Lee and his commanders determined to attempt a final assault the next morning, but, realizing the futility of the strategy, on the morning of April 9, 1865, Lee formally surrendered to Union General Ulysses S. Grant, effectively ending the Civil War. Interestingly, the two generals met to discuss the terms of the surrender at the home of Wilmer McLean, who had moved to Appomattox Court House from Manassas Junction to escape the war after the First Battle of Bull Run was fought in his fields.

ARLINGTON
NATIONAL CEMETERY

Robert E. Lee's Virginia home, just across the Potomac River from Washington, D.C., originally was the home of his wife, Mary Ann Randolph Custis, a descendant of George Washington's stepson. When Lee resigned his army commission, the property was seized by the Union army and turned into officers' headquarters and troop campgrounds for the soldiers defending the capital. In the summer of 1863, soon after the Battle of Gettysburg, the federal government confiscated the site and turned it into a much-needed military cemetery. The United States made a restitution payment of $150,000 to Lee's son in 1883 after the Supreme Court ruled that the government had obtained the property illegally.

ATLANTA, CAMPAIGN
AND SIEGE
(MAY 1-SEPTEMBER 2, 1864)

Atlanta, known as the "Gate City of the South" because of its importance in manufacturing and communications, was a prime target in the Union's war strategy. Major General William T. Sherman's goal for his Atlanta campaign was to sever all rail lines running to and from the city. In May 1864, his 100,000-man army began to move toward their goal from Chattanooga. Confederate General Joseph E. Johnston gathered his 62,000 troops at Dalton, Georgia; his aim was to defend the city and the Confederate supply lines by delaying Sherman's advance, perhaps until the November election, when it was hoped that Lincoln would be defeated by a candidate more sympathetic to the Southern cause. The two generals ended up in a kind of cat-and-mouse

game, with many small, vicious battles at such places as Snake Creek Gap, Resaca, Pine Mountain, and Kennesaw Mountain.

By July 4, Johnston had been forced to within seven miles of Atlanta, and was replaced by General John B. Hood, who attacked Sherman's approaching troops more aggressively, but no more successfully, than had his predecessor. Hood then established himself in Atlanta. The Battle of Atlanta was fought on July 22, but it did not deter Sherman's continued advance. He bombarded the city for over a month. A final Confederate effort, the Battle of Jonesboro, on August 31-September 1 failed to protect the remaining rail line south of the city, and Sherman was victorious. The Confederates evacuated Atlanta on September 2, 1864, but not before they destroyed its remaining supplies. When Sherman's forces marched into Atlanta on the following day, they found a ruined city.

BALTIMORE RIOT
(APRIL 19, 1861)

Some of the first blood shed in the Civil War was not in battle, but in a riot between civilians and Union soldiers. A week after Fort Sumter, secessionist feelings were running high in Baltimore, the largest city in Maryland, a border state. Because the railroad did not run through the city, rail cars had to be pulled by horses from the terminal at one end of town to the terminal on the other side of town. While a Northern regiment on its way to Washington was being transferred in this way, it was blocked by angry civilians. The soldiers were forced to continue on foot, and they were followed by a secessionist mob throwing bricks and stones. Some soldiers fired their guns into the crowd before they boarded their train; they left behind their marching band and a lot of their equipment. Four soldiers and 12 civilians were killed, and many were injured. Maryland authorities demanded that no more federal troops were to be routed through the state, and the mayor and police chief of Baltimore sanctioned the destruction of key railroad bridges to ensure that the demand was met. Federal troops occupied the city on May 13 and declared martial law. Baltimore was occupied for the entire war.

CLARA BARTON (1821-1912)

Massachusetts-born Clara Barton was the first female clerk in the United States Patent Office in Washington, D.C., when she began her one-woman soldiers' relief campaign in 1861. Beginning in July 1862, the indefatigable Barton took wagon trains of medicines and supplies to the battlefield. Called the "Angel of the Battlefield," she fixed meals, distributed supplies, and, despite her lack of medical training, nursed wounded soldiers and even provided emergency medical care

on the front lines of the war, in such battles as Cedar Creek, Second Bull Run, Antietam, Chantilly, and Fredericksburg. In 1864, she was appointed superintendent of nurses for the Army of the James, under General Benjamin Butler. At President Lincoln's behest, Barton oversaw a project that included corresponding with the relatives of missing and captured Union troops, compiling lists of the wounded, and identifying soldiers buried in mass graves. She spent four years on this undertaking, one result of which was the marking of 12,912 graves at Andersonville Prison.

In 1869, an exhausted Barton traveled to Switzerland. Instead of the rest that she had intended to take, however, she became active in the International Red Cross. When she returned to the United States, she founded the American Red Cross and served as its first president, from 1882-1904. She also was instrumental in the government's ratification of the Geneva Convention in 1882.

PIERRE GUSTAVE TOUTANT BEAUREGARD
(1818-1893)

Known as the "Hero of Sumter" because he commanded the opening attack of the war, General Pierre Gustave Toutant Beauregard was responsible for much of the winning Southern strategy at the First Battle of Bull Run. He assumed command during the Battle of Shiloh in April 1862 after the death of General Joseph Johnston and was responsible for two other important Confederate victories, on the Bermuda Hundred peninsula in May 1864 and in Petersburg one month later. Beauregard also designed the Confederacy's "Southern Cross" battle flag.

JUDAH PHILIP BENJAMIN
(1811-1884)

Judah Benjamin was perhaps the best-known Jewish-American politician of the Civil War era. He served in Jefferson Davis's cabinet throughout the war, first as attorney general, from February through September 1861, then as secretary of war until March 1862, when he was forced to resign because of numerous Confederate losses, and, finally, as secretary of state March 1862 through the end of the war. Although he was controversial and unpopular, Benjamin was generally acknowledged to be "the brains of the Confederacy." In May 1865, he fled the country to avoid arrest, going from the Bahamas to England, where he practiced law and wrote legal treatises.

MARY ANN BALL BICKERDYKE
(1817-1901)

"Mother" Bickerdyke was a Sanitary Commission field agent who served in 19 battles, often on the front lines, during the entire Civil War. Although she put enlisted men first and often defied army regulations, she also was a favorite of Union generals. Sherman sought her services for his Atlanta campaign and, in fact, permitted no other women in his battlefield hospitals; she rode at the head of her corps in the May 1865 Grand Review of the Armies. Bickerdyke did not forget the enlisted men after the war, either. She worked as a pension attorney to help them obtain veterans' benefits, long before she received her own pension in 1886.

BLACK CODES (1865-1866)

The precursors to the "Jim Crow" laws were enacted by Southern Democrats at the beginning of Reconstruction to limit the rights of freed slaves. Although the black codes varied in each state, in general they restricted the rights of African-Americans to buy, own, or sell property, to marry or make other legally binding contracts, to sit on juries, to own weapons, to vote or hold elected office, to travel without a pass and proof of residence, and to freely assemble; employment restrictions limited the professions open to blacks, established apprenticeship regulations, and required proof of steady employment. The black codes were struck down by the Radical Republicans, and from 1866 until 1877, voting and other legal rights were available to blacks in the South. The return of power to Southerners after Reconstruction paved the way for segregation and systematic discrimination, conditions that continued unabated until *Brown v. Board of Education* was decided by the United States Supreme Court in 1954.

JOHN WILKES BOOTH
(1838-1865)

John Wilkes Booth, one of the most popular actors of his day, was a fervent supporter of the Confederacy. In early 1865, he devised a plan to kidnap Lincoln and ransom him in exchange for Confederate prisoners. Lincoln's failure to appear at the site of the planned abduction and Lee's subsequent surrender at Appomattox Court House on April 9 led Booth to abandon this plan. He soon came up

with a new idea, to assassinate Lincoln, Vice President Andrew Johnson, General Ulysses S. Grant, and Secretary of State William Seward. His accomplices were unsuccessful, although Seward sustained severe knife wounds, but Booth entered Lincoln's box at Ford's Theater during a performance of *Our American Cousin* and shot him in the head. He then jumped from the box to the stage, leading some audience members to believe that his action was part of the play. Booth broke his leg but managed to escape on horseback to a barn owned by Richard Garrett near Front Royal, Virginia. On April 26,

he and one of his cohorts were discovered; their hiding place was set on fire and Booth was shot to death as he emerged from the burning building.

BORDER STATES

The border states of Delaware, Kentucky, Maryland, and Missouri were slave states that had large antislavery factions. Delaware had the fewest slaves and was the most loyal to the North. Maryland was much more divided, and federal troops occupied the state throughout the war, especially in its secessionist-leaning eastern portion. Kentucky and Missouri had pro-Confederate governors and pro-Union legislatures. Lincoln considered the border states so vital to the defense of the Union that he delayed issuing the Emancipation Proclamation until he was sure that these states would not secede.

BELLE BOYD (1843-1900)

Belle Boyd, known in the South as "La Belle Rebelle" and in the North as the "Secesh Cleopatra," was perhaps the most notorious Confederate spy. Her career as a spy began when she was seventeen, after she killed a Union soldier to protect her mother. She provided Stonewall Jackson with critical information about Union troop movements during his 1862 Shenandoah Valley campaign. Although she was imprisoned on several occasions, she continued her work undeterred. The first of Boyd's three husbands was a Union naval officer whose ship captured a blockade runner on which she was traveling. He let her escape, resigned his commission, and married her in England, where Boyd became an actress. Her memoirs were published in London in 1865. After she returned to the United States, she acted and gave popular dramatic lectures about her experiences. She died of a heart attack while on tour in Wisconsin.

MATHEW B. BRADY (1823-1896)

One of America's most famous portrait photographers, Mathew Brady set out to document the Civil War using wet-plate photography, which, unlike the daguerrotype process, allowed some mobility as well as the ability to reproduce pictures. With official authorization, but using his own funds, Brady and his 22 teams of photographers followed Union forces and took over 3,500 photographs.

Along with portraits of soldiers, civilians, and camp life, these photos documented every major battle of the war, Although many of these photographs were posed to enhance their dramatic effect, Brady's work provided the public with a vivid and shocking picture of the devastation of war.

BRAXTON BRAGG (1817-1876)

A brilliant military strategist but an indecisive leader, Confederate General Braxton Bragg was known for his harsh discipline of his troops and for turning seeming Confederate victories into stalemates or losses in the Battles of Perryville, Chickamauga, and Missionary Ridge.

JOHN BROWN (1800-1859)

Radical abolitionist John Brown was condemned as a lunatic by Southern whites and viewed as a hero-martyr in the North. Although he ran a station of the Underground Railroad in Richmond, Ohio, he believed that more overt action was required. On May 24, 1856, Brown, along with four of his sons and two other men, massacred five proslavery settlers near Pottawatomie Creek in Kansas, in retaliation for a raid on antislavery Lawrence. After spearheading other guerrilla attacks, Brown began to plot to lead a slave rebellion in the South and then to set up and govern a free black republic in the Appalachian

BULL RUN (MANASSAS), CAMPAIGN AND FIRST BATTLE OF (JULY 16-21, 1861)

Although neither the Confederate nor the Union army was yet battle-ready, by July 1861 both sides agreed that it was time for the war to begin; morale was high in both camps, and many believed that the war would be won swiftly and easily. The South wanted to prove its soldiers' superiority and the North wanted to prevent the Confederate Congress from convening in Richmond, Virginia, the new capital, at the end of July. More important, perhaps, most of the Union recruits had enlisted for three-month stints after Fort Sumter fell in April.

Union General Irvin McDowell, with a force of 30,000 men, intended to invade Virginia and reclaim Richmond, while Confederate General Pierre Beauregard's goal, with his army of 20,000 men, was to gain the right of peaceful coexistence for the Confederacy by a show of Southern strength. At the same time, Union General Robert Patterson's 18,000 soldiers were supposed to prevent Confederate

Mountains. To further his plans, Brown, along with a force of 22 men—five blacks and 14 whites, including three of his sons—seized the federal arsenal at Harpers Ferry, Virginia (now West Virginia), on October 16, 1859, and took control of the town. A patrol sent out to notify nearby blacks about the uprising brought back several hostages but was unable to recruit any slaves to the cause. Further, the ill-conceived scheme made no allowance for escape. On October 18, a contingent of marines from Washington, led by Robert E. Lee and Jeb Stuart, attacked the raiders, killing 10 of them, including two of Brown's sons, and captured Brown. Convicted of treason and murder, Brown was hanged on December 2 at Charlestown.

General Joseph E. Johnston's 12,000-member army near Harpers Ferry from joining Beauregard's troops. Although Union reconnaissance soldiers were forced back after a preliminary skirmish on July 18, when the main battle began on July 21, close to an important railroad line in Manassas Junction, near Bull Run creek, the North initially had an advantage because of its larger fighting force. However, the arrival of Johnston's contingent, which had evaded Patterson at Harpers Ferry, gave the South the advantage and turned the battle around, forcing the Union to beat a retreat to Washington, D.C., 25 miles to the east..

Hundreds of spectators had driven down from Washington with picnic lunches to observe this battle. Instead of the quick Union victory they came to see, the onlookers received a graphic lesson about the realities of war.

BULL RUN (MANASSAS), CAMPAIGN AND SECOND BATTLE OF (AUGUST 26- SEPTEMBER 1, 1862)

After the Seven Days and Peninsula campaigns, the Confederates had successfully defended Richmond but made no territorial gains. General Robert E. Lee wanted to move the fighting north of the Rappahannock River. His plan was to divide his troops; 24,000 men under General Stonewall Jackson would go to Manassas Junction to capture the Union supply depot, and 30,000 men would follow the next day, under his and General James Longstreet's command. Union General John Pope fought Jackson from August 28-30; mistaking a pull-back by Jackson for a retreat, Pope pursued Jackson, not realizing that his troops had been joined by Lee and Longstreet. The Confederate counterattack forced Pope's army to retreat to Washington.

JOHN CALDWELL CALHOUN
(1782-1850)

John C. Calhoun was a chief proponent of states' rights and was ardently proslavery. His "doctrine of nullification" held that state conventions, which had ratified the Constitution, also could declare any federal law unconstitutional and thus nullify it. This concept later was used by the Southern states to justify secession.

CARPETBAGGERS

During Reconstruction, many Northerners moved to the South, carrying their belongings in soft luggage known as carpetbags. They quickly took control of state and local governments and were notorious for their corruption. The term *carpetbagger* was used for years to describe any Northerner who lived in the South, regardless of motive.

CHANCELLORSVILLE, BATTLE OF (APRIL-MAY 1863)

In the spring of 1863, General Robert E. Lee, outnumbered by more than two to one and using the same strategy of dividing his forces that he had used at Second Bull Run, drove Union General Joseph Hooker's army north of the Rappahannock River. Hooker had planned to move against Lee's troops at Fredericksburg, striking at his left and rear flanks, but his army met with a surprise attack by General Stonewall Jackson on May 1 and withdrew to Chancellorsville. Ignoring scouting reports about Jackson's movements,

Hooker was unprepared for Jackson's attack on his right flank the next day. The Union forces defended their position for three days but finally were forced to retreat on May 5.

Although Chancellorsville was called "Lee's masterpiece," both sides paid heavily for this Confederate victory. Casualties numbered over 17,000 Union soldiers and almost 13,000 Confederates. Among the Southern casualties was Stonewall Jackson, who was shot accidentally by his own men during the fighting on May 2 and died on May 10.

CHATTANOOGA, CAMPAIGN AND BATTLE OF
(OCTOBER-NOVEMBER 1863)

Chattanooga, Tennessee, was the gateway to the southeastern Confederacy and thus was an important strategic prize. By early October 1863, General Braxton Bragg had cut off Union supply lines, leaving Union General William S. Rosencrans's troops in Chattanooga on the verge of starvation. General Ulysses S. Grant, recently appointed to command Western forces, replaced Rosencrans with General George H. Thomas and went on the offensive. By November 1, Union supplies once again began to arrive by steamboat on the Tennessee River.

As Grant planned to attack the Confederates who held Lookout Mountain and Missionary Ridge, vantage points that surrounded the city on the north, southeast, and southwest, Bragg was reorganizing his command, in part because a number of his corps commanders had requested to be transferred. The Battle of Chattanooga began with the fall of Lookout Mountain

in the "Battle Above the Clouds" on November 23-24. The next day, Union soldiers, acting without orders, routed the Confederates from Missionary Ridge. This win put the North in control of Chattanooga, and Tennessee, and made it possible for Union troops to move into Georgia and Alabama.

MARY CHESNUT
(1823-1883)

Mary Chesnut, the wife of United States Senator James Chesnut, the first senator to resign his office to join the nascent Confederate government, and a friend of Varina Davis, the Confederacy's First Lady, put her unique vantage point during the war to good use. She kept a detailed and insightful diary of the events and personalities of the Civil War that was published posthumously in 1905 as *Diary from Dixie;* a revised edition was published in 1949. In 1982, historian C. Vann Woodward won the Pulitzer Prize for his edition of the diary, which was retitled *Mary Chesnut's Civil War.*

CHICKAMAUGA, BATTLE OF
(SEPTEMBER 19-21, 1863)

Union soldiers, under the command of General William Rosencrans, occupied the strategically critical city of Chattanooga, Tennessee, in September 1863. They set off in pursuit of the Confederates after Southern General Braxton Bragg spread rumors that his troops were retreating; in reality, Bragg was gathering reinforcements in preparation

General Grant's army crossed this pontoon bridge during the Battle of Cold Harbor.

for an attempt to regain control of the contested city. Bragg pursued the Union troops to Chickamauga, Georgia, 15 miles south of Chattanooga. In the aftermath of a fierce and bloody battle that had a combined casualty rate of almost 30 percent, the Union forces retreated to Chattanooga, where Bragg's troops cut off virtually all of their supply lines. This was the South's last major victory in the war.

COLD HARBOR, BATTLE OF
(JUNE 3, 1864)

Considered to be Confederate General Robert E. Lee's last important field victory and Union General Ulysses S. Grant's biggest mistake, the Battle of Cold Harbor ended the month-long campaign that included the Battles of the Wilderness and Spotsylvania. Grant believed that he could win the war by destroying Lee's army in this tiny town eight miles from Richmond. Grant's troops were delayed, however,

COLONIZATION MOVEMENT

Prior to the Civil War, some Northern abolitionists and Southern slaveholders promoted the idea of settling emancipated slaves in foreign colonies. In 1822, the American Colonization Society bought land on the west coast of Africa and established Liberia; after 10 years, fewer than 1,500 emancipated slaves had settled there. In the 1850s, a group of Northern politicians, including Abraham Lincoln, endorsed an emancipation policy that would compensate former slaveowners for their lost "property" and resettle freed slaves in their African "homeland."

Lincoln's support for colonization continued after he was elected president. In August 1862, he asked black leaders to seek volunteers to settle an experimental colony in Central America, claiming that this was the best way to gain public acceptance of emancipation and to prevent prejudice and provide greater opportunities for blacks. Congress appropriated funds for the project and, in April 1863, over 450 free blacks set off for the new colony on Ile de Vache, off the Haitian coast; the site had been changed after a negative reaction from the governments of Honduras and Nicaragua. Private financial backing did not materialize, and hunger and disease devastated the colonists. The 368 survivors of the experiment returned to the United States in March 1864. Recognizing the vital contributions African-Americans were making to the Union war effort, the government attempted no further colonization schemes.

Grant at Cold Harbor.

which enabled the Confederates to dig a seven-mile-long trench between two rivers. The Union forces were shot down unit by unit as they made their frontal assault on the Confederate line. When Grant ended the assault half an hour later, the Union had sustained 12,500 casualties, 7,000 of them in the first minutes of the fighting.

COMPROMISE OF 1850

The Compromise of 1850 was a series of laws enacted to deal with the territory acquired after the Mexican War in a way that would appease pro- and anti-slavery forces. Under the Compromise, California was admitted to the Union as a free state and the territories of New Mexico and Utah were organized, but the slavery question was left for determination by their settlers. In addition, Texas's debts were cleared in exchange for abandonment of its claims to the New Mexico territory, the slave trade was prohibited in Washington, D.C., and the Fugitive Slave Act, which mandated the return of escaped slaves to their owners, was passed. Proslavery advocates alleged that the Compromise did not adequately protect the future of slavery, while Northerners were repelled by the harshness of the Fugitive Slave Act. Nevertheless, because of the Compromise of 1850, the Civil War was averted for another decade.

CONFEDERATE STATES OF AMERICA (C.S.A.)

The states that seceded from the United States to form the Confederacy were: Alabama, Arkansas, Florida, Georgia, Louisiana, Mississippi, North Carolina, South Carolina, Tennessee, Texas, and Virginia. Separate Confederate governments were established in the border states of Kentucky and Missouri, although they were officially members of the Union; because they also sent delegates to the Confederate Congress, the Confederate flag had 13 stars. The Confederate government was established in February 1861 in Montgomery, Alabama. The capital was moved to Richmond, Virginia, in May, where it remained until the city fell in April 1865, when the remnants of the Confederate government moved to Danville, Virginia. Jefferson Davis, of Mississippi, was the president of the Confederacy, and Alexander Stephens, of Georgia, was the vice-president. There was no Supreme Court. Restrictions in the Confederate Constitution on levying restrictive tariffs and financing internal improvements, along with the strong states' rights position of the states, meant that the Confederate government had more limited authority than did its Union counterpart.

Approximately nine million people lived in the Confederacy, more than a third of them slaves. The largely agriculture-driven Southern economy had a weak tax base; secession had left most of the wealth of the United States in the industrial North. When Union ships blockaded Southern ports of entry, the South was unable to obtain the imported food, clothing, and war supplies it so desperately needed, hastening the end of the Confederacy.

CONFISCATION ACTS (1861-1862)

The Confiscation Act of August 1861 authorized Union commanders in occupied territory to seize slaves who had performed war-related work for the Confederacy. These slaves were considered a "contraband of war," like any other Southern property. Although the so-called contrabands could be put to work for the Union cause, whether they were emancipated and what, if any, obligation the military had toward them, was not specified.

A more comprehensive Confiscation Act was passed in July 1862. This act authorized the seizure of Confederate supporters' property, including slaves, and mandated the emancipation of all seized slaves. Because slaveowners loyal to the Union were exempt from this law, Lincoln hoped that its passage might lead some Confederate states to rejoin the Union.

CONSCRIPTION

A shortage of volunteers led the Confederate Congress to pass the first draft law in America on April 16, 1862. All white men between the ages of 18 and 35 were conscripted for three years; the upper limit was raised to 45 in September. By February 1864, the age range was expanded to include men between 17 and 50 when the conscription of free blacks and slaves for such "auxiliary" services as manual labor also was authorized. On March 13, 1865, the Confederate Congress authorized the drafting of slaves for armed military service.

Conscription began in the North on March 3, 1863, when the Enrollment Act was passed by the United States Congress to draft men between the ages of 20 and 45 for three years of military service. The passage of this law set off antidraft riots.

A variety of exemptions, substitutions, or commutation fees were available to men who sought to avoid military service in either army. In both the North and South, the true goal of the conscription laws was to encourage volunteers to enlist.

COPPERHEADS

The Peace Democrats in the North who favored a negotiated peace with an independent Confederacy

were known as Copperheads. Accused of disloyalty and treason, the Copperheads formed societies such as the Knights of the Golden Circle, the Order of American Knights, and the Sons of Liberty. Lincoln arrested the most radical Copperheads, suppressed antiwar newspapers, imposed censorship, and suspended *habeas corpus*. Clement L. Vallandigham, one of the most prominent antiwar activists, was convicted of treason and exiled to the South.

CRATER, BATTLE OF THE (JULY 30, 1864)

A regiment of Pennsylvania coal miners built an explosive-filled mine shaft beneath a Confederate fort at Petersburg, Virginia, in July 1864. The tunnel, which was 511 feet long, was packed with four tons of gunpowder; the crater created by the explosion was 170 feet long, 70 feet wide, and 30 feet deep. Confederate units literally were blown into the air, and several regiments were buried by the blast. A delay in the Union attack, along with poor leadership, led to disaster for the Northern troops. Many of the soldiers jumped into the crater rather than advancing around it, and they became easy targets for the Southern forces that surrounded its rim. As a result of this Union fiasco, Grant put General Ambrose Burnside on extended leave and dismissed General James H. Ledlie, the commander of the division leading the attack, who had been drinking rum in a bomb shelter while his leaderless troops advanced.

GEORGE ARMSTRONG CUSTER (1839-1876)

Known primarily for "Custer's Last Stand" in the Battle of the Little Bighorn in 1876, George Armstrong Custer was a Union hero during the Civil War. Although he graduated last in West Point's Class of 1861, Custer became the Union's youngest general in June 1863, when he was 23 years old. He was involved in all but one of the major battles fought by the Army of the Potomac. Although he was wounded only once, 11 horses were shot out from under him during the course of the war.

JEFFERSON
FINIS
DAVIS
(1809-1889)

The son of a Revolutionary War veteran, and only a second-generation Southerner, Jefferson Davis was born on June 3, 1808, in Christian County (now Todd), Kentucky, not far from Abraham Lincoln's place of birth. His family relocated to Wilkinson County, Mississippi, several years later. Davis attended Transylvania University in

Kentucky and West Point, from which he was graduated in 1828. He spent the next seven years on the northwestern frontier and served in the Black Hawk War. In 1835, he eloped with Sarah Taylor, the daughter of his commander, Zachary Taylor, and resigned his commission. The Davises moved to Brierfield, a 1,000-acre cotton plantation in Mississippi. Within three months of their marriage, he and his wife came down with malaria, and she died. In 1845, Davis married Varina Howell; over the years, they had six children, two of whom were born while he was president.

Also in 1845, Davis entered politics, when he was elected as a Democrat to the United States House of Representatives. His political career was interrupted during the Mexican War in 1846, when he commanded the Mississippi Rifles, a volunteer regiment, in the battles of Monterrey and Buena Vista. On his return in 1847, the governor of Mississippi appointed Davis to a vacated seat in the United States Senate, where he was a vocal supporter of Senator John C. Calhoun during the debates about the Compromise of 1850. He resigned from the Senate in 1850 to run for governor, but was defeated. Returning to politics in 1853 as President Franklin Pierce's secretary of war, Davis was reelected to the Senate in 1857. He was not a secessionist, but he was a strong supporter of states' rights and slavery. After Lincoln was elected president, Mississippi seceded from the Union and Davis resigned his Senate seat.

Although he had hoped to be appointed to a military command, Jefferson Davis became the provisional president of the Confederate States of America, by vote of the Confederate Congress, and was sworn in on February 18, 1861; he was elected to a six-year term by popular vote on November 9, 1861, and was inaugurated on February 22, 1862. Davis tried to industrialize the agriculture-based Southern economy and to gain foreign support for the new nation. His military knowledge enabled Davis to choose his generals well, but his interference in military affairs led five secretaries of war to resign. As the war went on, many critics accused Davis of becoming increasingly dictatorial, an especially strong condemnation in a nation based on the concept of states' rights, and he faced stiff resistance from his cabinet and the Confederate Congress.

On May 10, 1865, Davis was captured at Irwinsville, Georgia. He was indicted for treason and imprisoned at Fort Monroe for two years but was never brought to trial. He published a defense of the South, *The Rise and Fall of the Confederate Government*, in 1881 and died in 1889 at Beauvoir, his home in Biloxi, Mississippi.

VARINA HOWELL DAVIS

(1826-1905)

Varina Howell Davis, the first lady of the Confederacy, was Jefferson Davis's second wife. She was suspected of Union sympathies, in part because her grandfather had been an eight-term governor of New Jersey and because she had been educated in Philadelphia. Criticized for her lavish entertaining—and also for not entertaining enough to keep up her

besieged nation's morale—and derided for interfering in political matters, she was her husband's confidante, nurse, and defender, and put aside her own political views to further his career. She had six children, two of them during the war; a five-year-old son died in 1864 after falling from a balcony of the Confederate "White House." Davis was with her husband in May 1865 when he was captured, and she lobbied for two years for her husband's release, even pleading his case with President Johnson. After Jefferson Davis's death in 1889, she converted Beauvoir, their home near Biloxi, Mississippi, to a home for Confederate veterans. She published her memoirs in 1890, moved to New York City to live with her daughter, and wrote for magazines until she died in 1905.

DECLARATION OF CAUSES
(DECEMBER 24, 1860)

The Declaration of Causes was the written explanation and justification of South Carolina's reasons for seceding from the Union.

MARTIN ROBINSON DELANY
(1812-1885)

The first African-American officer in the Civil War was Martin Robinson Delany, a Union army surgeon who achieved the rank of major. Delany, who was a Harvard-trained physician, a journalist, and a social activist, was active with the Underground Railroad and wrote for an abolitionist newspaper owned by Frederick Douglass. He had a strong interest in tracing his African heritage and, in the 1850s, was a proponent of the colonization movement that encouraged free blacks to resettle in Africa. In 1865, Delany spearheaded the fight for equal pay for black soldiers.

DOROTHEA DIX
(1802-1887)

In June 1861, after spending over 20 years as a social reformer working to improve conditions in prisons and mental institutions, Dorothea Dix was appointed superintendent of women nurses for the Union army. To help convince opponents that women could do the job, she formulated the Dix Plan for Nurses, under the terms of which army nurses could be only plain-looking women over the age of 30 who adhered to a strict dress code requiring black or brown dresses and no hoops or jewelry. Throughout the war, more than 3,000 women served under "Dragon Dix," who worked without pay and who often paid nurses from her own money because the government had not allocated any funds for paying them.

DIXIE

The South was popularly referred to as Dixie. The most likely explanation for this nickname is that it comes from the Mason-Dixon Line, the political boundary between North and South. "Dixie" also was the title of the unofficial Confederate anthem.

STEPHEN ARNOLD DOUGLAS
(1813-1861)

Stephen Douglas's political career moved rapidly, from prosecuting attorney in 1835, to the Illinois legislature in 1836, to the Supreme Court of Illinois from 1841 to 1843, to the United States House of Representatives in 1843, and to the United States Senate in 1847. Known as the "Little Giant," he was a proponent of the Kansas-Nebraska Act of 1854, which repealed the Missouri Compromise and left the question of slavery in the territories up to the people who lived there, a concept known as popular, or squatter, sovereignty.

Douglas, a Democrat, ran for reelection to the Senate in 1858 against the Republican candidate, Abraham Lincoln. During the seven Lincoln-Douglas debates, Douglas advocated popular sovereignty as a peaceful way to settle the slavery question, while Lincoln argued for a unified stand against slavery. Douglas narrowly won the Senate election, but his 1860 candidacy for president split the Democratic ticket, putting Lincoln in the White House. When war was declared, Douglas became an early and avid supporter of Lincoln and the Union, stating that "[t]here can be no neutrals in this war, only patriots—or traitors." He contracted typhoid fever and died in 1861.

FREDERICK DOUGLASS
(1817-1895)

Frederick Augustus Washington Bailey was born in Maryland to a slave mother and an unknown white father in 1817. Sent to work as a house slave in Baltimore when he was eight years old, he learned to read and write with the help of his owner's wife. In 1838, on his second attempt, he escaped to New Bedford, Massachusetts, and changed his name to Douglass. At an 1841 meeting of the Massachusetts Anti-Slavery Society, he spoke about his experiences as a slave and as a black man facing prejudice in the North. William Lloyd Garrison, the head of the society, hired him to lecture across the country and raise support for the abolitionist movement.

In 1845, after publishing his autobiography, *Narrative of the Life of Frederick Douglass*, and fearing that he would be arrested as a runaway slave, Douglass went to England, where he lectured and raised enough money to buy his freedom. In 1847,

Douglass moved to Rochester, New York, and founded an antislavery newspaper, the *North Star*, which, along with its successor, *Douglass's Monthly*, provided an important outlet for abolitionist views for more than 16 years. He continued to fight for equal rights for blacks, and used his home as a station on the Underground Railroad.

Although he was not a radical abolitionist, Douglass tried to make slavery the prime focus of the Civil War. He proposed that if morality was not a strong enough reason for ending slavery, the Union should support abolition to destroy the Southern economy. He also worked to recruit African-American soldiers for the Union, and to obtain equal treatment and pay for them.

After the war, Douglass was appointed to several government positions, including consul general to Haiti from 1889 to 1891. Throughout his life, he continued to revise and expand his autobiography, publishing *My Bondage and My Freedom* in 1855, and *Life and Times of Frederick Douglass* in 1881. He died at home in Washington, D.C., in 1895.

DRAGOONS

Traditionally, the cavalry fought from horseback, while the infantry fought on foot. Dragoons combined the two types of warfare, riding their horses to battle and using them for mobility on the field, but dismounting to fight. With few exceptions, the cavalry units of the Civil War technically were mounted infantrymen, or dragoons.

DRED SCOTT DECISION
(MARCH 1857)

Dred Scott was a slave who had lived with his owner, an army surgeon, in Illinois and the Minnesota territory from 1834-1838. They returned home to Missouri and, after his master died in 1843, Scott brought suit for his and his family's freedom in the Missouri courts, based on his temporary stay in a free state and free territory. The case ultimately landed in the United States Supreme Court, which ruled 6-2 against Scott. *Dred Scott v. Sandford* held that slaves and their dependents could not bring lawsuits because they were not citizens of the United States or of Missouri, that Scott's status as a slave was determined by his residence when he brought suit and not by his stay in free territory, and that the Missouri Compromise was unconstitutional under the Fifth Amendment. This was the first decision since *Marbury v. Madison* in 1803 in which the Court declared an act of Congress unconstitutional. *Dred Scott* intensified the growing division between North and South.

JUBAL ANDERSON EARLY
(1816-1894)

General Jubal "Old Jube" or "Jubilee" Early, a Virginian who originally opposed secession, went on to become a respected commander in the Confederate Army. An 1837 graduate of West Point, Early served in the Seminole and Mexican Wars. After leaving the military, he became a lawyer and lawmaker, but he returned to his military roots with the outbreak of the war. He participated in many major battles, from First Bull Run and Antietam through Gettysburg and the Wilderness. In 1864, Early led a raid on Washington, D.C. He levied a $200,000 fine on Frederick, Maryland, and burned Chambersburg, Pennsylvania, when its citizens refused to pay $500,000. Ultimately defeated by Union General Philip H. Sheridan in the Shenandoah Valley in March 1865, he was relieved of his command.

Early traveled to Mexico, Cuba, and Canada, and he wrote his memoirs. Returning to Virginia in 1869, he again practiced law. A staunch defender of the Confederacy even after the war, Early became the first president of the Southern Historical Society.

EPHRAIM ELMER ELLSWORTH
(1837-1861)

On May 24, 1861, Union Colonel Elmer Ellsworth ripped down a Confederate flag that was flying over the Marshall House Tavern in Alexandria, Virginia, and was shot at point-blank range by the irate owner of the hotel, becoming the first officer to die in the Civil War. He was the leader of a regiment of New York firefighters, the Fire Zouaves, who had come to Washington to defend the capital. Before the war, Ellsworth had studied law under Lincoln. He also had organized the Chicago Zouaves and traveled the country presenting drill exhibitions, including a presentation on the White House grounds in August 1860.

EMANCIPATION PROCLAMATION
(JANUARY 1, 1863)

The original goal of the Civil War was to reunite the divided nation, not to eradicate slavery. Lincoln feared that freeing the slaves would lead the border states to secede. As the war went on and Southern victories continued to mount, however, the beneficial impact of slavery on the South's war effort became more apparent. In July 1862, Congress passed the second Confiscation Act, which freed all Confederate slaves who were in Union territory. On September 22, 1862, five days after the Union victory at Antietam, Lincoln issued a preliminary Emancipation Proclamation warning the Confederate states that if they did not return to the Union by January 1, 1863, he would free all of their slaves. The South was predictably outraged, but reaction to the proclamation in the North was mixed. Abolitionists and Radical Republicans foresaw the end of slavery, but others believed that wholesale emancipation would lead to massive unemployment and social unrest. The final Emancipation Proclamation was issued, as promised, on New Year's Day 1863.

Because slave states in the Union and under Union

control, such as Tennessee and parts of Virginia and Louisiana, were excluded under the terms of the decree, no slaves actually were freed as a direct result of the Emancipation Proclamation, but it did have other significant effects. Strong antislavery sentiment in Britain and France meant that they could not support the Confederate cause when slavery became the major issue of the conflict, despite their dependence on Southern cotton. The Emancipation Proclamation also led to the official end of slavery throughout the United States, by means of the Thirteenth Amendment to the Constitution, which took effect on December 18, 1865.

54TH MASSACHUSETTS REGIMENT

The most famous African-American regiment to fight in the Civil War was organized in February 1863, just after the Emancipation Proclamation, by the Massachusetts Governor John Andrew, an abolitionist. Under the command of white officers, led by Colonel Robert Gould Shaw, the 650 black volunteers fought for their civil rights as well as for the Union. They refused to accept any pay, and some refused to obey orders, because black soldiers were paid at a significantly lower rate than were white soldiers. After Governor Andrew appealed unsuccessfully to the secretary of war for equal pay for the unit and was informed that pay rates were established by the Militia Act of 1862, he solicited private and state funds to make sure that the unit was compensated equally with whites.

The 54th Regiment was sent to South Carolina where, on July 10, 1863, they led the effort to capture Battery Wagner, a heavily armed fort that was key to the recovery of Fort Sumter and the capture of Charleston. Forty percent of the unit, including Colonel Shaw, died in this Union massacre. Although the bravery of the 54th garnered respect for black soldiers, official recognition did not come quickly. In 1901, Sergeant William Carney of the 54th Massachusetts Regiment was the first of 23 African-Americans who had fought in the Civil War to receive the Congressional Medal of Honor.

DAVID GLASGOW FARRAGUT
(1801-1870)

David Glasgow Farragut served in the navy from the time he was nine years old and was a midshipman during the War of 1812. As an adult, he settled in Norfolk, Virginia, but he moved his family to the North at the beginning of the Civil War. His first major command during the war came in December 1861, when he was named to lead the West Gulf Blockading Squadron. Under his leadership, the squadron captured New Orleans on April 24, 1862, as well as Baton Rouge, Natchez, and Port Hudson. He also took Galveston and other Texas ports, but was unable to capture one of the

biggest prizes, Vicksburg. On August 5, 1864, Farragut braved the heavily mined Mobile Bay, where he uttered his famous battle cry, "Damn the torpedoes! Full speed ahead!" Farragut's victory at Mobile Bay closed Mobile's harbor to blockade runners. In December 1864, he was promoted to vice admiral, a rank that had been created for him, and in 1866, he became the first naval officer in the United States to be named a full admiral.

NATHAN BEDFORD FORREST
(1821-1877)

A self-made man with little formal education, Nathan Bedford Forrest was a real estate baron, cotton planter, and slave trader before the war. Following his own advice to "Get there first with the most men," he became a well-regarded Confederate cavalry officer, rising from private to lieutenant general. Forrest fought at Fort Donelson in February 1862 and covered the Confederate retreat from Shiloh two months later. He was known for conducting lightning raids that destroyed rail and telegraph lines and captured Northern arms and forts. During the fighting for Union-held Fort Pillow, Tennessee, in April 1864, Forrest allegedly led his troops in the massacre of over 200 unarmed soldiers—most of them black—who already had surrendered. Two months later, he had one of his greatest triumphs when his unit routed a Union force more than twice its size from Brice's Cross Roads, Mississippi, and, in the process, captured numerous small arms, artillery, and supply wagons. Union General William T. Sherman considered Forrest to be "the most remarkable man our Civil War produced on either side." After the war, the financially-ruined Forrest went into the railroad business. He is generally believed to have been the first Grand Wizard of the Ku Klux Klan, in 1867, although he later resigned from the group because of its terrorist nature.

FORT HENRY AND FORT DONELSON, CAMPAIGN
(FEBRUARY 1862)

A combination of naval and land forces commanded by General Ulysses S. Grant captured Fort Henry, on the Tennessee River, on February 6, 1862, marking the first step in the Union's invasion of the South. Grant's troops camped at Fort Henry until the night of February 11, when they began to move toward their next target, Fort Donelson, 12 miles to the east on the Cumberland River. Union gunboats were defeated by the Southern forces on February 14, but inept Confederate leadership allowed Grant's land forces to prevail. When Confederate General Simon Bolivar Buckner, requested the terms of surrender, Grant informed him that "No terms except an unconditional and immediate surrender can be accepted," giving rise to his nickname, "Unconditional Surrender" Grant. On February 16, approximately 15,000 Confederate soldiers surrendered. With the capture of these two western Tennessee strongholds, the North ensured that Kentucky and western Tennessee would remain in the Union and gained an invasion route to the South.

FORT PILLOW, BATTLE OF
(APRIL 12, 1864)

Fort Pillow, about 40 miles north of Memphis, Tennessee, was responsible for protecting Union navigation along the Mississippi River and thus was an inviting target for the South. The fort was held by 262 black soldiers and 295 white soldiers. On April 12, 1864, 1,500 Confederate soldiers led by General Nathan Bedford Forrest surrounded and attacked the fort. When the

Interior View of **FORT SUMTER** *on the 14th April 1861.*
after its evacuation by Maj. Robert Anderson, *1st Artt U.S.A. Comdg*
Showing the north end of West Barracks, with the two tiers of Casements and
Barbette of adjacent north channel face.

Union commander refused to surrender, they stormed the fort. Northern casualties were high—230 killed, most of them black, 100 wounded, 168 whites and 58 blacks captured. Accounts of the battle are conflicting; the Northern view is that the Confederate troops, shouting racial epithets, massacred the Northerners in cold blood after they had surrendered, while the Southern account claims that the North's refusal to surrender led to the fighting that caused the casualties.

FORT SUMTER
(APRIL 12-14, 1861)

The Civil War began on April 12, 1861, when Confederate forces fired on Fort Sumter, a Union-held garrison on an island in the harbor at Charleston, South Carolina. After South Carolina seceded from the Union, it demanded the withdrawal of Union forces from Charleston. Major Robert Anderson moved his contingent of fewer than 100 soldiers from Fort Moultrie to the more secure Fort Sumter. By preventing the relief ship *Star of the West* from entering the harbor on January 9 to deliver supplies and reinforcements, Confederate forces severely weakened this conspicuous but vulnerable symbol of the Union. At 4:30 AM on April 12, General Pierre G. T. Beauregard directed his soldiers to begin shelling the garrison. Thirty-four hours later, Anderson surrendered. Union troops withdrew from Fort Sumter at noon on April 14, returning to New York by steamship. No blood was shed during the siege, but two men died and one was seriously wounded as the result of an explosion during the midpoint of the Union's hundred-gun salute to its flag. Anderson was present on April 14, 1865, when this same flag was once again raised over Fort Sumter, exactly four years after its surrender, and only a few hours before Lincoln was assassinated.

FRANKLIN, BATTLE OF
(NOVEMBER 30, 1864)

Confederate General John Bell Hood attempted a daring—and foolhardy—direct attack against the Union line, under General John Schofield, at Franklin, 15 miles south of Nashville. His goal was to retake Tennessee and then move on to Virginia and destroy Grant's army. Over the strong objections of his subordinate officers, Hood launched the attack at 3:30 PM on November 30, 1864. By the time the fighting ended less than six hours later, little except bloodshed had been achieved. Hood lost at least a quarter of his troops and at least six of his generals were killed. Schofield moved on toward Nashville, relatively unscathed.

FREDERICKSBURG,
CAMPAIGN AND BATTLE OF
(NOVEMBER-DECEMBER 1862)

In the wake of Antietam, Lincoln replaced McClellan with a reluctant General Ambrose E. Burnside. Burnside planned to attack Richmond by way of Fredericksburg, a major railroad junction 45 miles north of the Confederate capital. By November 19, Burnside's 120,000 troops were positioned across the Rappahannock River from Fredericksburg. However, they could not move against their target because the pontoons they needed to bridge the river had not yet arrived. Even after the pontoons arrived, Burnside delayed the attack for another three weeks, giving Lee ample opportunity to organize his 75,000 soldiers. The Union army

Confederate dead at Fredericksburg.

finally attacked on December 13. The focus of the battle was a heavily defended ridge at Marye's Heights; crossing the frozen fields beneath the hills, Union fighters made easy targets for Confederate guns. The fighting continued from morning through evening, resulting in more than 12,500 Union and 5,000 Confederate casualties. Burnside planned to lead a further attack the next morning, but his officers convinced him to rethink his strategy. The Union army retreated on December 15. Northern morale sank after the Battle of Fredericksburg, and Burnside was relieved of his command at his own request.

FREEDMEN'S BUREAU

Congress established the Bureau of Refugees, Freedmen, and Abandoned Lands on March 4, 1865, to provide emancipated slaves with the means to become self-reliant. Funded by the Department of War and led by General Oliver O. Howard, the 900 agents of the Freedmen's Bureau distributed food and clothing to emancipated slaves, tried to establish a racially equitable judicial system, and built medical clinics. The Freedmen's Bureau established a land-grant program to distribute confiscated or abandoned Confederate land to ex-slaves; about 3,500 of the four million eligible freed slaves ultimately received the "forty acres and a mule" promised under this program. Education was another area of activity for the Freedmen's Bureau. With the assistance of Northern charities, the bureau established thousands of schools for African-Americans, ranging from evening classes and private schools to the Hampton Institute and Atlanta, Fisk, and Howard Universities.

Plagued by a reputation for corruption among its agents and by allegations that it was merely a tool for power-hungry Republicans, the Freedmen's Bureau had a rocky existence but continued to work for civil rights for blacks until it was officially disbanded in 1872.

JOHN CHARLES FRÉMONT
(1813-1890)

John Charles Frémont already was a national hero by the time the Civil War began. Known as the "Pathfinder" because of his explorations in the West, he represented California in the Senate and, in 1856, became the fledgling Republican Party's first presidential candidate. In May 1861, Lincoln appointed him to command the army's Western Department. More flamboyant and less militarily qualified than most of Lincoln's generals, Frémont issued his own emancipation proclamation on August 30, 1861, which declared martial law in Missouri, ordered the confiscation of all property owned by secessionists, and freed their slaves. Lincoln, concerned about maintaining Union support in the pro-slavery border states, rescinded the proclamation and removed Frémont from his command. Political pressure led Lincoln to reappoint him to head the new Mountain Department in West Virginia in March 1862. Frémont's forces were defeated by Confederate General Stonewall Jackson in the Shenandoah Valley campaign, and he resigned his command rather than serve under General John Pope, a former subordinate, after a military reorganization.

FUGITIVE SLAVE ACT

Enacted as part of the Compromise of 1850, the Fugitive Slave Act was intended to calm the slavery debate but instead fueled it. The federal fugitive slave law enacted in 1793, which required runaway slaves to be returned to their owners, was not followed by the 1840s. Personal liberty laws in the North gave fugitive slaves increased opportunities to oppose their return, and the Underground Railroad and other "vigilance committees" helped slaves to escape. The Fugitive Slave Act of 1850 was Congress's response to Southern demands for a stricter federal law. Under this law, U.S. marshals were required to participate in the capture and return of escaped slaves. Anyone who protected or assisted a runaway slave was subject to six months in prison and a fine of $1,000 plus the market value of the slave, and an accused fugitives had no right to trial or even to testify on his or her own behalf. Commissioners who administered the law accepted affidavits from Southern courts or statements of white witnesses as proof of ownership and received $10 for each slave returned to the South, but only $5 if the fugitive was exonerated. In the North, moderate and militant abolitionists joined forces to oppose the new law, and the Underground Railroad grew more active. Blacks moved by the thousands to Canada because the lack of a statute of limitations in the law meant that blacks who had lived in free states for more than 20 years were being arrested. The Fugitive Slave Act was responsible for returning more than 300 fugitives to slavery. The Supreme Court upheld the constitutionality of the law in 1859, and it was not repealed until June 1864.

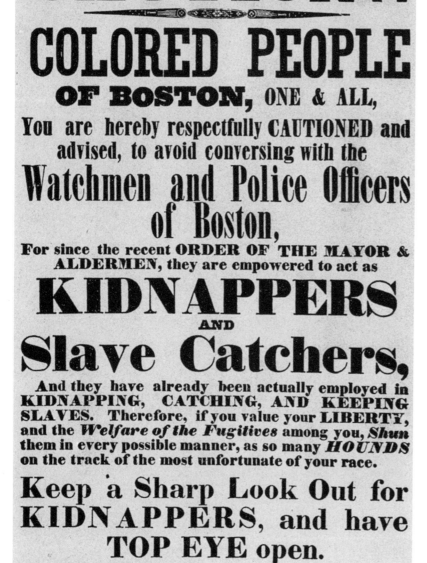

GARIBALDI GUARD

The so-called Garibaldi Guard was an Italian-American regiment from New York City, the 39th New York Infantry. Founded by Francesco Casale, the regiment included many men who had served with the Italian patriot Giuseppe Garibaldi and who believed that the Union cause represented the same republican ideals of freedom and justice that Garibaldi had fought for in Italy. The Garibaldi Guard was distinguished by its members' red shirts, which they wore in homage to their freedom-fighting hero.

WILLIAM LLOYD GARRISON

(1805-1879)

An indefatigable reformer, William Lloyd Garrison worked for women's suffrage, civil rights, and prohibition, but he is best known for his fierce opposition to slavery. Viewing the abolitionist cause as a moral crusade, Garrison created a public forum for his opinions when he established *The Liberator* in 1831; he continued to publish this influential abolitionist newspaper for 35 years, until slavery was abolished by the Thirteenth Amendment. In 1832, he founded the New England Anti-Slavery Society, which worked for immediate emancipation. Garrison refused to vote while the government sanctioned slavery and did not support the Civil War until Lincoln issued the Emancipation Proclamation.

GENERAL ORDER NO. 11
(DECEMBER 17, 1862)

The infamous "Anti-Jew Order" of December 17, 1862, one of the most notoriously anti-Semitic documents in United States history, was issued in response to the profiteering that developed after a limited cotton trade was reinstituted between a select group of Northern merchants and Southern planters. When speculation in cotton intensified to the point that it interfered with military performance, Western regional commander General Ulysses S. Grant needed a scapegoat and, because many merchants in the area were Jewish, he blamed Jewish traders for the situation; ironically, several of the Jewish merchants had received their trading permits when Grant's father had interceded on their behalf with his son. Acting through Assistant Adjutant General John A. Rawlins, he issued General Order No. 11. Under the terms of the order, all Jews were expelled from the region, which encompassed such towns as Paducah, Kentucky, and Holly Springs and Oxford, Mississippi, places where Jewish soldiers were stationed under Grant's command. Representatives of the Jewish community took their protest directly to the President. On January 1, 1863, Lincoln ordered General Henry Halleck, Grant's superior officer, to rescind General Order No. 11, pointing out the impropriety of singling out "an entire religious class, some of whom are fighting in our ranks." Grant rescinded the order on January 4, without acknowledgment or apology.

GETTYSBURG ADDRESS
(NOVEMBER 19, 1863)

Contrary to common belief, Lincoln did not write the 270-word Gettysburg Address on the back of an envelope as he rode the train on his way to the dedication of a national military cemetery at the Gettysburg battlefield. Rather, he wrote the speech in Washington, D.C., and revised it after he arrived in Gettysburg. Lincoln delivered the Gettysburg Address on November 19, 1863. He was finished in two minutes, before many in the audience realized what he was saying and before the photographers had sufficient time to take his picture at the podium. Public reaction to the speech was divided along party lines, and Lincoln himself felt that the speech was a failure. He continued to revise it, however, and it is the fifth, and final, revision that appears on the Lincoln Memorial.

GETTYSBURG, BATTLE OF
(JULY 1-3, 1863)

The Battle of Gettysburg, a major turning point for the North, was a bloody victory, with over 23,000 casualties out of a Union force of 85,000, as well as over 20,000 Southern casualties out of a force of 70,000. The battle began almost by accident, when Confederate troops, who were encamped west of Gettysburg, Pennsylvania, went into the town on July 1 seeking to replenish their supply of shoes. Union cavalry soldiers camped southwest of the town saw the Southerners and immediately readied themselves for battle. The Confederates then prepared to attack the Union line. Outnumbering the North three to two, the Confederates won the first day of battle. By the morning of July 2, however, the Union army had regrouped into

a hook-shaped formation on the hills surrounding the town. General Robert E. Lee took the offensive but was unable to breach Union General George Meade's defense during fighting in a peach orchard, a wheatfield, a mass of boulders later nicknamed "Devil's Den," Culp's Hill, Cemetery Ridge, and Little Round Top, a hill south of the town. The next day, the fighting continued at Culp's Hill and Cemetery Ridge. Pickett's Charge, about 15,000 soldiers led across an open field by General George E. Pickett, was the South's desperate final effort to gain Cemetery Ridge; several Confederates reached the top of the hill. Although he attained one of his objectives—to move the fighting out of Virginia— Lee failed to meet his second goal of a major victory that could gain foreign support for the South. The Confederacy's second, and last, invasion of the North was over. Lee's army began its retreat to Virginia on July 4.

GRAND REVIEW OF THE ARMIES (MAY 23-24, 1865)

The 80,000 men of General George Gordon Meade's Army of the Potomac and the 65,000 troops of General William Tecumseh Sherman's Army of Georgia, as well as the civilian workers, medics, and freed slaves who had followed Sherman on his March to the Sea, celebrated the end of the war by marching in a victory parade before President Andrew Johnson, General-in-Chief Ulysses S. Grant, government officials, and almost the entire population of Washington, D.C., on May 23-24, 1865. The volunteer armies were disbanded following the review.

ULYSSES SIMPSON GRANT (1822-1885)

Chronically unsuccessful at business but a military genius, Ulysses S. Grant was one of the greatest generals of the Civil War. Born Hiram Ulysses Grant in Ohio in 1822, his name was changed due to a mistake made by the congressman who recommended him for West Point. After his graduation in 1843, Grant served in the Mexican War and was stationed at forts across the country, from New York to Michigan to the Oregon Territory. He married Julia Dent in 1848, with whom he had four children. While stationed at Fort Humboldt, California, Grant grew depressed over his separation from his family and began to drink heavily. To avoid a court-martial, he resigned his commission on April 11, 1854; rumors of drunkenness persisted throughout his career. During the next six years, Grant tried and failed at a succession of jobs, from farming and peddling

firewood to working in the U.S. Customs House and in his father's leather goods store.

When the Civil War began, Grant volunteered for service. He rose through the ranks, establishing a reputation as an aggressive warrior and a quick thinker. Although he was beaten by the Confederates at Belmont, Missouri, on November 7, 1861, he became a Union hero known as "Unconditional Surrender" Grant after he captured Fort Henry and Fort Donelson in February 1862. His next win, at the Battle of Shiloh, Tennessee, was more controversial and resulted in heavy losses. Lincoln refused to replace him, however, arguing that "I can't spare this man—he fights!" Grant was responsible for the successful campaign to capture the Confederate stronghold of Vicksburg, Mississippi, which was surrendered on July 4, 1863. In October 1863, Lincoln appointed Grant to command all Western forces. On March 12, 1864, after his victories at Chattanooga, Lookout

Mountain, and Missionary Ridge, Lincoln named Grant General-in-Chief of the Armies of the United States. Coordinating all the Union armies, Grant, leading Meade's army, pursued a strategy of "relentlessly pounding" Lee's army through the Battles of the Wilderness, Spotsylvania, Cold Harbor, and the siege of Petersburg; at the same time, Sherman and Sheridan were ravaging the Confederates in Georgia and the Shenandoah Valley. These campaigns came at a great cost in terms of lives lost on both sides, but "Grant the Butcher" succeeded in destroying the Confederate army. Lee accepted Grant's generous terms of surrender at Appomattox Court House, Virginia, on April 9, 1865.

After the war, Grant served briefly as Johnson's secretary of war. Grant became president in 1868 and served for two terms, but the leadership skills that served him so well during the war did not translate to politics. Although Grant himself was honest, his administration was riddled with corruption. Business failures continued to plague Grant after he left office. He completed the *Personal Memoirs of U. S. Grant* only a few days before he died of throat cancer on July 23, 1885; published by Mark Twain, Grant's autobiography earned literary accolades and almost a half a million dollars for his family.

HORACE GREELEY
(1811-1872)

Through his editorials in the *New York Tribune*, which he founded in 1841, Horace Greeley became an important national opinion-maker before and during the Civil War. A supporter of protective tariffs, organized labor, prohibition, and westward expansion— "Go West, young man" was his famous advice to the

unemployed—Greeley also was an ardent abolitionist. Although his opinions about the war changed frequently and unpredictably, he always promoted immediate emancipation, and his writings helped to broaden Northern support for abolition. In the spring of 1864, Greeley spearheaded a peace conference in Canada with Confederate agents. Criticized for its failure, Greeley met with additional censure after the war when he posted bail for Jefferson Davis and advocated a general amnesty for former members of the Confederacy. Despite the criticism, however, Greeley maintained enough popular support to be nominated by a coalition of Democrats and Liberal Republicans to run for president against Grant in 1872. Greeley died less than a month after Grant's resounding victory.

GREENBACKS

Congress passed the Legal Tender Act in February 1862 to finance the North's continually escalating need for money for the war, which was costing the North approximately $2.5 million a day by the end of that year. By July, the government had issued the nation's first national currency, $400 million in noninterest-bearing notes; these treasury notes were backed only by the government's promise to pay, not by gold or silver. The reverse side of the notes was printed in green ink, giving rise to the name *greenbacks*. The value of the greenbacks rose and fell with the Union army's victories and defeats; at their low point, greenbacks were worth about 35 cents. In February 1863, in response to these fluctuations, Congress passed the National Banking Act, which established a national bank system that was empowered to issue notes of uniform value.

ROSE O'NEAL GREENHOW
(?-1864)

Rose O'Neal Greenhow used her position as a leader of Washington society and her wide circle of friends as a front for her spying activities for the Confederacy. She notified General Beauregard about the plans for the first Bull Run campaign. After her arrest on August 23, 1861, her home was turned into a women's prison. A string of security breaches at "Fort Greenhow" led to her imprisonment in the Old Capitol Prison in January 1862. She was released that spring and sent to the South, where she was treated as a hero. Running the blockade, she went to France, where she met with Napoleon III, and then to England, where she was presented to Queen Victoria. Before returning home, she wrote a memoir, *My Imprisonment.* She drowned on September 30, 1864, off the coast of Wilmington, North Carolina.

HABEAS CORPUS, SUSPENSION OF

Article I of the United States Constitution guarantees that citizens will not be imprisoned without just cause, unless "in cases of rebellion or invasion the public safety may require it." The writ of *habeas corpus* ensures that there will be a court hearing to determine whether there is sufficient reason to hold a prisoner for trial. In April 1861, Lincoln suspended *habeas corpus* and arrested the secessionist activists who led the Baltimore Riot. Chief Justice Taney ruled that only Congress had the authority to suspend this basic right. Lincoln ignored this ruling and authorized the military to arrest anyone showing "substantial and unmistakable complicity" with the rebels; this "complicity" encompassed sympathizing with the South as well as treason, resulting in the arrests of hundreds of political prisoners. Congress demonstrated its approval of Lincoln's actions by passing the *Habeas Corpus* Act in March 1863. Throughout the war, an estimated 13,000 to 18,000 Copperheads, pacifists, newspaper editors, peace activists, and other Northern dissenters were held without trial. Although Jefferson Davis initially scoffed at Lincoln's actions, at various times throughout the war he, too, suspended the writ of *habeas corpus* and declared martial law in certain areas of the Confederacy.

HENRY WAGNER HALLECK
(1815-1872)

Henry "Old Brains" Halleck served as the general-in-chief of the Union Armies from 1862 until 1864, when he was replaced by Grant and given the newly created position of chief of staff. After graduating from West Point in 1839, Halleck served in the Mexican War but spent much of his career writing and translating military and law books.

Halleck was appointed to replace General John Charles Frémont in Missouri in 1861 and oversaw the Union victories at Forts Henry and Donelson and at Nashville. In the aftermath of the Shiloh campaign in the spring of 1862, he forced Confederate General P.T.G. Beauregard to retreat but failed to follow through with a vigorous pursuit. Because of his reputation for extreme caution, the generals who served under Halleck often disregarded his orders or tried to get around them. For instance, Grant began to move toward Vicksburg before notifying Halleck, his superior officer, of his plans; by the time Halleck's refusal of the strategy arrived, the campaign was too far along to abort. A cautious and hesitant strategist, Henry Halleck was far better qualified for administrative duties than for a battlefield command.

HANNIBAL HAMLIN
(1809-1891)

Hannibal Hamlin was Lincoln's vice president during his first term, from 1861 through early 1865. He began his political career as a Democrat, serving in the Maine legislature and then in Congress, in the House of Representatives from 1843 to 1847 and in the Senate from 1848 to 1857. In 1856, his antislavery views led him to switch his affiliation and join the new Republican Party. Elected Governor of Maine that same year, he soon resigned to take a seat in the Senate, where he served from 1857 until 1861. When he was nominated to be Lincoln's running mate in the 1860 election, Hamlin's opponents focused on his dark coloring and abolitionist stance and claimed that he was trying to pass as white. Radical Republican Hamlin was dropped from the ticket in the 1864 election, and replaced by Democrat Andrew Johnson. In 1869, he returned to the Senate as a supporter of Reconstruction. Hamlin was appointed minister to Spain in 1881.

HAMPTON ROADS CONFERENCE
(FEBRUARY 3, 1865)

On February 3, 1865, a peace conference was held aboard the *River Queen*, a steamship anchored in the James River at Hampton Roads, Virginia, the site where the *Monitor* and the *Merrimac* had battled three years earlier. A newspaper editor, Francis P. Blair, Sr., arranged the conference after he met informally with Confederate President Jefferson Davis. The Union was represented by President Abraham Lincoln and Secretary of State William Henry Seward, and the Confederacy was represented by Vice President Alexander H. Stephens, Senator Robert M. T. Hunter, and Assistant Secretary of War John A. Campbell. The four-hour meeting ended in a stalemate, with Lincoln refusing to recognize Confederate sovereignty and the South refusing to agree to the abolition of slavery.

HARPERS FERRY

Control of Harpers Ferry, Virginia (now West Virginia), the site of John Brown's raid of October 16-18, 1859, bounced back and forth between the North and the South throughout the war. Union forces abandoned the arsenal on April 18, 1861, after setting fire to the machine shops and destroying a cache of 17,000 muskets. By June 18, the Confederates confiscated the remaining supplies and sent them to Southern arsenals, where they were used for ordnance production. The

Harpers Ferry, the site of John Brown's raid.

Confederates then abandoned the town, which was occupied by Union troops until it was captured by General Stonewall Jackson on September 15, 1862, but it reverted to Union control after Lee's defeat at Antietam two days later. In July 1863, during the Gettysburg campaign, Harpers Ferry was captured by the Confederates and recaptured by the Union yet again. It remained under Union control for much of the remainder of the war.

HEROES OF AMERICA

Like the Copperheads in the North, members of the Southern secret society known as the Heroes of America were antiwar activists. Also known as the "Red Strings" because of the insignia they wore on their lapels, they discouraged enlistment, opposed the draft, and sought reunification with the North. They also encouraged and protected deserters, worked with and as spies, and assisted escaped prisoners of war. Members of the Heroes generally were not property owners, and they considered the war "a rich man's war and a poor man's fight."

HORSE ARTILLERY

An innovation that made it appear that an army was much larger than it actually was, the horse artillery comprised small cannons, such as howitzers, that could be easily assembled and packed onto horseback. This mounted, or "Mountain," artillery could be taken into rocky terrain that would otherwise restrict the use of larger weapons.

JULIA WARD HOWE
(1 8 1 9 - 1 9 1 0)

Writer, lecturer, peace activist, abolitionist, and suffragist Julia Ward Howe edited the antislavery newspaper *The Commonwealth* with her husband, Samuel Gridley Howe, but she is best known for writing the "Battle Hymn of the Republic." Howe was inspired to write the poem after she attended a troop review near Washington, D.C., on November 18, 1861. Published in the *New York Herald Tribune* on January 14, 1862, and in the *Atlantic Monthly* in its February edition, Howe's words, sung to the tune of "John Brown's Body," became the Union's most popular anthem.

IRON BRIGADE OF THE WEST

The Iron Brigade of the West was composed of spirited young men from Wisconsin, Michigan, and Indiana who were anxious to prove themselves as soldiers. Also called the Black Hat Brigade, the Iron Brigade earned its name, along with a reputation for fearlessness, at Second Bull Run, Antietam, Fredericksburg, and Chancellorsville. More than 65 percent of the unit was lost at Gettysburg, and the brigade never regained its eagerness for action.

IRONCLADS

The Civil War marked the first time that iron-armored ships were used in battle. Less seaworthy than wooden ships, ironclads were well suited to battles in rivers and bays. The Union blockade of Southern ports relied largely on the traditional wooden ships that made up its fleet; however, early in the war the North did maintain one ironclad, the USS *Monitor*. Because the Confederacy had few ships, it turned to more modern shipbuilding methods. Less industrialized than the North, however, the South had to scavenge for materials. It salvaged the *Merrimac*, an abandoned Union frigate, covered it with iron armor, and rechristened it the CSS *Virginia* (although it continued to be referred to by its former

name). The *Monitor* and the *Merrimac* fought the first battle of steam-powered ironclads on March 9, 1862, and demonstrated the increasing importance of armored ships.

Wooden ships remained the standard in both navies, but by the time the war ended, the Union had 58 ironclads and the Confederacy had 21. Confederate ironclads included the CSS *Arkansas*, used in the Vicksburg campaign, the CSS *Albemarle*, used in 1864 in North Carolina, and the CSS *Tennessee*, which tried to hold off Farragut's fleet in the Battle of Mobile Bay. Union ironclads included the USS *Tecumseh*, which was destroyed during the Battle of Mobile Bay, and the USS *New Ironsides*, an ocean-going cruiser involved in the 1865 assault on the South's only remaining open port, Fort Fisher, North Carolina. European navies also began to add ironclads to their fleets after the ships proved their worth in battle during the Civil War.

THOMAS JONATHAN "STONEWALL" JACKSON
(1824-1863)

Known for his bravery, his strong religious convictions, his attention to military detail and discipline, and his ability to inspire great loyalty among his men, Thomas Jonathan "Stonewall" Jackson was one of the Confederacy's most important generals. He grew up in rural Virginia, graduated from West Point in 1842, and served in the Mexican War, where he first met Robert E. Lee. Leaving the army in 1851, Jackson spent the next 10 years teaching philosophy and artillery techniques at the Virginia Military Institute. His first marriage, to Elinor Junkin, ended after a year with his wife's death in 1854. He married Mary Anna Morrison in 1857.

Jackson joined the Confederate Army in 1861 and was sent to Harpers Ferry, where he organized a 4,500-man brigade. In July, at the First Battle of Bull Run,

Jackson and his brigade earned the nick-name "Stonewall" for their bravery in holding their line against a fierce enemy attack. Stonewall Jackson's reputation for military brilliance skyrocketed in the aftermath of the Shenandoah Valley campaign in the spring of 1862, when his 17,000 troops defeated a Union force of more than 60,000 men. Jackson suffered a major setback in the Seven Days campaign, but his victories at the Second Battle of Bull Run, Antietam, and Fredericksburg restored his reputation.

Stonewall Jackson's greatest victory, at Chancellorsville on May 1, 1863, was also his last. On May 2, he was mistakenly shot by his own men. His left arm was amputated, which caused Lee to comment: "He has lost his left arm; but I have lost my right arm." Jackson developed pneumonia and died on May 10, 1863.

JEWISH - AMERICANS IN THE CIVIL WAR

Jewish-Americans fought on both sides during the Civil War and generally were treated no differently than any other soldiers. Some Jews, such as Confederate Secretary of State Judah Benjamin, rose to national prominence. However, anti-Semitism was not unknown. The most blatant example was Grant's infamous General Order No. 11, which blamed Jewish traders for disruptive and corrupt cotton speculation and expelled all Jews from the area under his control

in Tennessee, Kentucky, and Mississippi; almost immediately, Lincoln demand-ed that he rescind the order.

ANDREW JOHNSON
(1808-1875)

Andrew Johnson was born into poverty North Carolina and set-tled in Tennessee in 1826, working as a tailor. His wife, Eliza, taught him to read, and in 1830 he entered local politics. By 1847, he was elected to Congress, and he became a senator 10 years later, serving as Governor of Tennessee in the interim. He unsuccessfully sought the Democratic presidential nomination in 1860. Johnson was the only Southern senator who maintained his seat in Congress, even after Tennessee seceded in June 1861. Lincoln appointed him military governor of Tennessee in March 1862. His performance in that position, along with ticket-balancing considerations, led him to be nominat-ed as Lincoln's running mate in 1864 by a coalition of War Democrats and Republicans, on the Union-Republican ticket. When Lincoln was assassinated on April 14, 1865, Johnson became president.

As president, Andrew Johnson tried to implement Lincoln's plans for a lenient Reconstruction but was faced with continual power struggles with the Republican-dominated Congress. When he fired Secretary of War Edwin Stanton in violation of the Tenure of Office Act, a law that Johnson believed to be unconstitutional, the House of Representative brought 11 counts of impeachment against him on February 24,

1868. Although Johnson was the first president to be impeached, he was not convicted; the Senate tally was one vote short of the number required for removal. On Christmas Day 1868, Johnson issued a complete amnesty for all former Confederates who remained unpardoned, and in 1869 he pardoned three men who remained imprisoned for their participation in Lincoln's assassination. Johnson ran for the Senate in 1869, and for the House in 1872; these were the only two elections he lost. He ran again for the Senate and won in 1875, becoming the only former president to serve as a senator, but he died four months into his term, on July 31, 1875.

ALBERT SIDNEY JOHNSTON
(1803-1862)

Albert Sidney Johnston was reputedly the best soldier to fight for the South. An 1826 graduate of West Point, the Kentucky-born Johnston established his military reputation in the Black Hawk War and the Mexican War. Between the wars he settled in Texas, where he fought in the war for independence and served as secretary of war from 1838 until 1840. When the Civil War began, Johnston was stationed in California, as commander of the Department of the Pacific. Offered a Union commission, Johnston's loyalty to Texas led him to choose to fight for the Confederate cause. After his forces lost Forts Henry and Donelson, Tennessee, to Grant in February 1862, General A. S. Johnston moved on to the Shiloh campaign. Shot in the leg on April 6, 1862, during the first day of the Battle of Shiloh, Johnston bled to death before anyone realized how severely he had been wounded.

JOSEPH EGGLESTON JOHNSTON
(1807-1891)

Joseph Eggleston Johnston of Virginia graduated from West Point in 1829 and fought in the Seminole War and the Mexican War. Stationed in Kansas during the 1850s, he was appointed quartermaster general of the U.S. Army in 1860. Johnston commanded the combined Confederate forces at the First Battle of Bull Run in July 1861. Named a full general in August, Johnston protested that he had not received the correct seniority, which was the first of many disputes he had with President Jefferson Davis. Davis, who believed that Johnston's defensive tactics indicated an unwillingness to fight, refused to approve the general's strategies; the two men blamed each other for the Confederate losses at Vicksburg, Chickamauga, and Chattanooga. Given command of the Army of Tennessee in December 1863, Johnston developed a strategy to deflect Union General William T. Sherman's advance toward Atlanta, but Davis

wanted to pursue a more aggressive stance and relieved him yet again in July 1864. In February 1865, General J. E. Johnston returned to command the Carolinas campaign. Although Davis ordered him to continue fighting, Johnston surrendered to Sherman on April 26, 1865.

After the war, Johnston went into the insurance business, served one term in Congress, was a railroad commissioner, and wrote his memoirs. He died in 1891 of pneumonia he contracted while serving as a pallbearer at Sherman's funeral.

JOINT COMMITTEE ON THE CONDUCT OF THE WAR
(1861-1865)

Congress established the Joint Committee on the Conduct of the War to investigate early Union battle losses. Under the leadership of Senator Benjamin Wade of Ohio, its investigations quickly took on political overtones and the committee became an important tool of the Radical Republicans. The committee supported those generals who agreed with its ostensibly patriotic agenda, even incompetent ones like Joseph Hooker and Benjamin Butler, and focused its investigations on more politically conservative generals, especially George McClellan. Continuing for several months after the war ended, the committee advised President Andrew Johnson to enact a punitive Reconstruction policy.

KANSAS-NEBRASKA ACT (1854)

Sponsored by Stephen Douglas and enacted by Congress in 1854 in apparent contradiction of the terms of the Missouri Compromise of 1820, the Kansas-Nebraska Act divided part of the Louisiana Purchase into the territories of Kansas and Nebraska and provided that popular sovereignty, or the will of the people, would resolve whether these territories would enter the Union as slave or free states. Passage of the act paved the way for a violent five-year border war in the territory of Kansas. The territory became known as "Bleeding Kansas" because of such events as John Brown's 1856 massacre at Pottawatamie. The Kansas-Nebraska Act led to the formation of the Republican Party and brought the issue of slavery to the forefront of national debate.

PHILIP KEARNY
(1816-1862)

Philip Kearny, "the most perfect soldier" according to General Winfield Scott, was a graduate of Columbia University. After joining the army, he was sent to France to study cavalry tactics, and he fought in Algeria in 1840. On his return, he fought in the Mexican War and lost his left arm in battle; after the loss of his arm, he would ride into battle clutching his horse's reins in his teeth. Kearny resigned his commission and returned to France, where

he won the Legion of Honor for his role in the Italian Wars. Appointed a general in the Union army in 1861, Kearny distinguished himself in the Peninsula campaign in the spring of 1862 and at the Second Battle of Bull Run the following August. Philip Kearny was killed at Chantilly on September 1, 1862, when he refused to surrender after riding accidentally into enemy lines. Because of his admiration for Kearny, Robert E. Lee called a truce to allow the fallen soldier to be returned to Union custody

KENNESAW MOUNTAIN, BATTLE OF (JUNE 27, 1864)

The Battle of Kennesaw Mountain, Georgia, was one of the bloodiest confrontations between Union General William T. Sherman and Confederate General Joseph E.

Johnston during the Atlanta campaign. Literally fighting an uphill battle as they charged up the rocky, heavily defended mountainside, the Northern troops were unable to dislodge the Southern line. After three assaults and heavy losses of personnel, the battle was a costly loss for the Union. Although he had won the battle, Jefferson Davis believed that Johnston was not sufficiently aggressive and removed him from his command in July.

"KING COTTON DIPLOMACY"

By 1860, the South produced nearly one billion pounds of raw cotton per year, approximately three-quarters of the world's supply. Because the textile industries in England and France depended on American cotton, the Confederacy presumed that those countries would take its side during the Civil War, and perhaps even provide military assistance. Based on this presumption, the South instituted a cotton embargo.

This belief in the supremacy of "King Cotton" proved to be misplaced. The growth of the Egyptian and Indian cotton industries, along with stockpiles of American cotton sufficient to last for a year, protected England and France from feeling the immediate effect of the embargo. When cotton supplies started to dwindle, in late 1862, it was the unemployed mill workers, not the power brokers, who suffered. European crop failures in the early 1860s made Northern corn and wheat much more valuable commodities than Southern cotton. The enactment of the Emancipation Proclamation provided the final blow to the South's strategy by adding a moral dimension to the economic considerations. Abandonment of the embargo came too late, however. Although the Confederacy desperately needed to fund its war efforts, it had voluntarily given up its major source of revenue. The Union blockade was firmly established, preventing the South from its belated attempts to trade cotton for much-needed war supplies.

KNIGHTS OF THE GOLDEN CIRCLE

The Peace Democrats in the North, also known as the Copperheads, formed secret societies to carry out their antiwar activities. These organizations, similar to the Confederate group known as the Heroes of the South, were especially active in Ohio, Illinois, and Indiana. The major Copperhead society was the Knights of the Golden Circle, which changed its name in late 1863 to the Order of American Knights, and again in 1864, to the Sons of Liberty.

LAND MINES

Land mines were used for the first time at Yorktown, Virginia, during the Peninsula campaign in May 1862. Confederate General Gabriel James Rains developed this innovative use of explosives, which initially was considered "unsporting" and even unethical by both North and South. Later in the war, however, both sides made use of land mines and booby traps.

FITZHUGH LEE (1835-1905)

Shot in the chest by an arrow at point-blank range early in his military career, Confederate General Fitzhugh "Fitz" Lee defied the odds and survived, going on to have successful careers in the military and in politics. Lee resigned his commission in the Union army in 1861, following the secession of Virginia. During the Civil War, he took part in the Peninsula campaign, Jeb Stuart's ride around McClellan, Antietam, Chancellorsville, Gettysburg, and Spotsylvania Court House. At the Battle of Winchester on September 19, 1864, he had three horses shot out from under him and sustained severe chest wounds. Returning to active service in January 1865, Lee fought in the Petersburg campaign. Following the Confederate surrender at Appomattox Court House, he attempted to lead his troops to North Carolina to aid General Joseph Johnston; realizing the futility of this move, he surrendered at Farmville, Virginia, on April 11, 1865.

After the war, Fitzhugh Lee became a farmer, businessman, and politician. He served as governor of Virginia from 1886 until 1890 and was appointed consul general to Havana, Cuba, in 1896, during the tumultuous period leading up to the Spanish-American War in 1898. The former Confederate general rejoined the Union army during that war, retiring as a brigadier general in 1901. In addition to his military and political successes, Fitzhugh Lee wrote *General Lee*, an acclaimed biography of his famous uncle, Robert E. Lee, that was first published in 1894.

ROBERT EDWARD LEE
(1807-1870)

Robert Edward Lee, one of the most respected figures in American history, was born on January 19, 1807, into a prominent Virginia family. The son of Revolutionary War commander Henry "Light-Horse Harry" Lee, he was raised by his mother, Anne Carter Lee, after his father fled to the West Indies as a result of business setbacks. Robert E. Lee graduated second in his class from West Point in 1829 and was assigned to

the Corps of Engineers, where he served for more than 15 years. He married Mary Ann Randolph Custis, Martha Washington's great-granddaughter, with whom he had seven children; all three of their sons became Confederate officers during the Civil War. Lee served on General Winfield Scott's personal staff during the Mexican War and played a key role in the capture of Veracruz. In 1852, Lee became the superintendent of West Point, where he expanded the curriculum to include courses in strategy. In 1855, he was promoted to lieutenant colonel and assigned to the Texas frontier.

Lee was visiting his family at Arlington, outside of Washington, D.C., in 1859 when he was assigned to stop John Brown's raid on Harpers Ferry. After arresting Brown and successfully completing his mission, Lee returned to Texas.

After Texas seceded from the Union in 1861, Lincoln, on Scott's recommendation, offered Lee command of the Union army. Although Lee opposed both slavery and secession, his loyalty to Virginia led him to resign his commission and join the Confederate army, where he first served as a military advisor to Jefferson

Davis. On June 1, 1862, after General Joseph E. Johnston was wounded at the Battle of Seven Pines, Lee took command of his army, which he renamed the Army of Northern Virginia. Outnumbered by Union troops on several fronts, Lee decided to consolidate his entire force and to move against one threat at a time. In June 1862, in the Battle of the Seven Days, Lee's army forced Union General George B. McClellan to retreat from Richmond, and, in August 1862, the Army of Northern Virginia defeated Union General John Pope at the Second Battle of Bull Run. Lee continued to move northward, dividing his troops before reuniting for a final attack. Stonewall Jackson's division captured Harpers Ferry, but Lee's advance was halted at the bloody Battle of Antietam on September 17, 1862, and he retreated to Virginia. In December 1862, Lee won a decisive victory at Fredericksburg, Virginia, and again in the spring of 1863, at Chancellorsville. Lee then moved north into Pennsylvania, but the Confederate defeat at Gettysburg in July 1863 changed the course of the war. Lee fought General Ulysses S. Grant in the Wilderness campaign in the spring of 1864 and was forced to retreat to Richmond and Petersburg. Lee became general-in-chief of all Confederate armies in February 1865, but it was too late. Richmond fell in April, and Lee surrendered to Grant at Appomattox Court House on April 9, 1865.

Barred from holding public office under the terms of the Proclamation of Amnesty and Reconstruction, Lee applied for a complete individual pardon, but his written oath of allegiance to the United States was lost, and the pardon was denied. Lee regained his right to vote in 1868, but his full citizenship was not restored until 1975, following the discovery of the missing oath at the National Archives five years earlier. Lee became the president of Washington College in Lexington, Virginia, where he established the first business and journalism schools in the country. Robert E. Lee died on October 12, 1870. After his death, Washington College was renamed Washington and Lee University.

WILLIAM HENRY FITZHUGH LEE
(1837-1891)

Like his father, Robert E. Lee, William Henry Fitzhugh "Rooney" Lee's loyalty to Virginia was stronger than his anti-secessionist beliefs. Rooney Lee served under General Jeb Stuart and participated in all of Stuart's rides around McClellan. He fought at Second Bull Run, in the Antietam campaign, at Fredericksburg, and at Chancellorsville. Injured early in the Gettysburg campaign during the Battle of Brandy Station, on June 9, 1863, and sent home to recover, Rooney Lee was taken prisoner. Although he was under threat of death, Robert E. Lee refused to authorize a one-for-one prisoner exchange, on the ground that he could not treat his son differently from any other soldier in his command. Included in one of the war's last prisoner exchanges, in March 1864, General Rooney Lee returned to the fighting; second in command of the Virginia cavalry, he was the only senior cavalry officer present when Lee surrendered to Grant at Appomattox Court House. After the war, Rooney Lee became a farmer, a state legislator, and a U.S. Representative. He died on October 15, 1891.

ABRAHAM LINCOLN

(1809-1865)

Born in Hardin County, Kentucky, on February 12, 1809, raised on the Indiana frontier, and largely self-taught, Abraham Lincoln was known for his honesty, integrity, and hard work. These qualities, along with his ability as a storyteller and a natural talent for leadership, pointed the way to a career in politics. After a brief stint of military service in the Black Hawk War of 1832 and several unsuccessful attempts at establishing a business in New Salem, Illinois, Lincoln was elected as a Whig to the first of four terms in the Illinois legis-

lature in 1834. He became a member of the state bar in 1836 and quickly became one of the most successful lawyers in Springfield. For six months each year, Lincoln worked as a "circuit lawyer," traveling through 15 counties, an area of about 8,000 square miles. He married Mary Todd in 1842; they had four sons, but only Robert, the eldest, lived to adulthood. In 1840, Lincoln campaigned throughout Illinois for the Whig presidential candidate, William Henry Harrison. His hope of being rewarded with the Whig Congressional nomination was not met, but he continued to work for the party and campaigned for Henry Clay in 1844. Elected to Congress on the Whig ticket in 1846, he served one term before returning to his law practice.

Returning to political office after the passage of the Kansas-Nebraska Act in 1854, Lincoln led the state legislators who opposed the spread of slavery into the territories before resigning from the legislature and running unsuccessfully for a Senate seat. In 1856, he joined the Republican Party and made more than 100 speeches on behalf of its presidential nominee, John C. Frémont. Lincoln was the Republican candidate for the United States Senate in 1858, running against the Democratic incumbent, Stephen A. Douglas. During the hard-fought campaign, Lincoln challenged Douglas to a series of seven debates on the issue of extending slavery into free territory. Douglas defended the popular sovereignty viewpoint of the Kansas-Nebraska Act, while Lincoln, who believed slavery to be "a moral, social, and political evil," argued that the Supreme Court's *Dred Scott* decision would allow slavery into all the territories. Although Douglas was reelected, the Lincoln-Douglas debates brought Lincoln to national attention. He was the Republican presidential candidate in 1860 and won the election, defeating a divided field that included Northern Democrat Stephen Douglas, Southern Democrat John C. Breckinridge, and Constitutional Unionist John Bell.

The South viewed Lincoln's election as the end of its political power in the federal government and, by the time he was inaugurated on March 4, 1861, seven Southern states had seceded from the Union. The Civil War began little over a month later, with the Confederate capture of Fort Sumter. Lincoln assumed broad war powers and proved to be adept at military strategy. His primary concern throughout the Civil War was to preserve the Union, not to abolish slavery. This moderate approach was important to prevent the border states from seceding and resulted in greater popular support for the war throughout the North. Only when the Northern military position was secure did Lincoln issue the Emancipation Proclamation. Although no slaves were freed

directly as a result of the proclamation, it added a moral element to the war's goals that brought European support and renewed purpose for the Union cause. As the fighting continued and Confederate victories mounted, however, a second Lincoln administration appeared unlikely until a run of Northern military victories during the summer of 1864 turned the tide of the war. Lincoln was reelected, solidly defeating the Democratic challenger, General George B. McClellan. Soon after his second inauguration, the war ended.

Lincoln had envisioned a reconciliation with the South conducted "with malice toward none; with charity toward all," but this vision was not realized after his

assassination on April 14, 1865. With Lincoln's death, Reconstruction was left to the control of the Radical Republicans.

ASSASSINATION OF ABRAHAM LINCOLN

Abraham Lincoln was the first American president to be assassinated. While attending a performance of *Our American Cousin* at Ford's Theater on April 14, 1865, John Wilkes Booth shot Lincoln in the head. He died less than 10 hours later, at 7:22 a.m. on April 15. Booth, who broke his leg when he jumped onto the stage after the shooting, escaped but was killed by federal troops on April 26, when he was discovered hiding in a barn near Port Royal, Virginia.

Initially intended to be a kidnapping in which Lincoln would be held hostage in exchange for the release of Confederate prisoners, Booth had changed his plan after Lee's surrender at Appomattox Court House. The new plot, conceived as an act of revenge for the defeat of the Confederacy, involved the murders of Lincoln and other highly placed government officials.

Although Booth masterminded the assassination, he did not act alone. Lewis Paine inflicted serious injuries on Secretary of State William H. Seward. George Atzerodt was assigned to kill Vice President Andrew Johnson, but never attempted to do so. David Herold accompanied Booth to Virginia; when Booth was killed, he surrendered. Mary E. Surratt owned the boardinghouse in Washington, D.C., where the conspirators met to make their plans. John H. Surratt, her son, who was to have killed Ulysses S. Grant, was in Canada on April 14 and later escaped to Italy; he served with the Papal Guards until he was recognized and returned to the United States in 1867 for trial, which resulted in a hung jury. Samuel Arnold and Michael O'Laughlin assisted in the planning, Edward Spangler held the horse Booth used to escape, and Dr. Samuel A. Mudd set Booth's broken leg.

All of the co-conspirators, except John Surratt, were captured, tried, and convicted by a military tribunal in proceedings that began on May 10 and lasted for six weeks. Atzerodt, Herold, Paine, and Mary Surratt were hanged on July 7. Arnold, Mudd, and O'Laughlin were sentenced to life imprisonment, and Spangler received a six-year sentence. O'Laughlin died of yellow fever in 1867. President Johnson, believing that the conspiracy was the work of former Confederate leaders, pardoned Arnold, Mudd, and Spangler in 1869.

MARY TODD LINCOLN
(1818-1882)

Mary Todd was born in Lexington, Kentucky, but moved to Springfield, Illinois, when she was 21 to live with her sister. Active and popular in political society, she married Abraham Lincoln in November 1842. They had four sons, but only Robert, the eldest, lived to adulthood. The politically ambitious Mary Todd Lincoln was not popular in Washington society because of her haughtiness and her tempestuous personality. Although she vowed her loyalty to the Union, she also was suspected of having Southern sympathies because of her Southern roots and because a number of her relatives fought for the Confederacy. Mary Todd Lincoln was at her husband's side when he was assassinated. Always emotionally unstable, the deaths of her husband and children took their toll; she was declared insane and was committed to a sanitarium for several months in 1875. She returned to her sister's home in Springfield, where she died on July 16, 1882.

JAMES LONGSTREET
(1821-1904)

Confederate General James "Old Pete" Longstreet graduated near the bottom of his class at West

Spy balloons being inflated in Washington, D.C. using Lowe's gas generators.

Point in 1842. Not effective as an independent commander, he was considered an excellent corps commander. Robert E. Lee referred to Longstreet as "my old war horse" and held him in the same esteem as Stonewall Jackson. Longstreet was not an aggressive fighter and preferred to take defensive positions. His delay in attacking on the second day of the Battle of Gettysburg and his reluctance the next day to begin Pickett's Charge, which he believed was doomed to failure, led some Southerners to blame him for the Confederate loss at Gettysburg and, ultimately, for losing the war. Lee's faith in him continued, however, and they were together during the surrender at Appomattox Court House.

After the Civil War, Longstreet was an insurance executive and a cotton factor. In a move that shocked many in the South, he joined the Republican Party. He was appointed minister to Turkey in 1880. Longstreet published his memoirs, *From Manassas to Appomattox,* in 1896 and was a U.S. railroad commissioner from 1898 until he died in 1904.

THADDEUS SOBIESKI COULINCOURT LOWE
(1832-1913)

Professor Thaddeus Sobieski Coulincourt Lowe, the "Father of the U.S. Air Force," was arrested as a Union spy when a hot-air balloon he had flown from Cincinnati, Ohio, landed nine hours and 900 miles later in Unionville, South Carolina, soon after the fall of Fort Sumter. The charges were dropped when he convinced his captors of his innocence, but as soon as he was released, he offered to spy for the Union army. He served as Lincoln's chief of army aeronautics from 1861 until 1863. During this time, Lowe and his crew conducted more than 3,000 reconnaissance flights over Confederate territory. The Confederate army also had an aeronautics program, headed by Captain E. Porter Alexander, but it was more limited in scope.

STEPHEN RUSSELL MALLORY
(1813-1873)

Secretary of the Navy Stephen Russell Mallory, the only Confederate cabinet member who kept his position throughout the war, was responsible for creating a navy for the Confederacy with few resources and little support from his government. Born in Trinidad and raised in Key West, Florida, Mallory served in the Seminole War from 1835 until 1840. He was elected to the United States Senate in 1850, where he chaired the Committee on Naval Affairs from 1855 until he resigned in January 1861, following Florida's secession. When he joined the Confederate cabinet, the South's navy consisted of ten ships. After Virginia seceded in April 1861, the Norfolk Navy Yard was taken over by the Confederacy and became a major resource, providing shipbuilding supplies, a dry dock and factory, 11 wooden ships, and the ironclad ship, the *Merrimac*. Mallory attempted to buy additional ships from the North, Canada, and Europe, but he knew that he could not hope to match the size of the established Union navy. Instead, he focused on developing newer, more powerful technologies, such as ironclads, torpedoes, and submarines. On April 2, 1865, after the fall of Richmond, Mallory was among the cabinet members who went to Georgia with President Davis. He was arrested and imprisoned at Fort Lafayette for ten months. In 1867, he received a full pardon from President Johnson and returned to practice law in Pensacola, Florida, until his death on November 12, 1873.

MANASSAS

Many Civil War battles had alternate names because, in general, the Confederacy named battles for the towns nearest to where they were fought, while the Union used the names of nearby rivers or bodies of water. Thus, the Battles of Bull Run also are known as the Battles of Manassas, especially in the South.

MASON-DIXON LINE

Between 1763 and 1767, the English astronomers Charles Mason and Jeremiah Dixon surveyed the boundary between Pennsylvania and Maryland to settle a border dispute. The line they established came to be seen as the dividing line between the North and the South during the Civil War.

GEORGE BRINTON MCCLELLAN
(1826-1885)

Union General George Brinton McClellan earned high honors at the University of Pennsylvania and went on to West Point by the time he was he was 16, where he graduated second in the class of 1846 and was voted "most likely to succeed." After distinguished service in the Mexican War, he taught engineering at West Point from 1848 until 1852, when he was transferred to the West. In 1855, he was sent to report military methods used in the Crimean War. McClellan resigned his commission in 1857 and became a railroad executive. When the Civil War began, he commanded the troops that ran the Confederate forces out of the area that was soon to

become West Virginia. Lincoln put him in command of the Army of the Potomac after First Bull Run. From November 1861, following General Winfield Scott's retirement, until March 1862, "Young Napoleon" McClellan was the general-in-chief of the Union armies. After he was removed as general-in-chief, he retained command of the Army of the Potomac. Although he excelled at training his forces, he had a reputation for arrogance and for being reluctant to move against the enemy. On several occasions he refused to attack, claiming that his troops were outnumbered when he actually had the advantage; his reliance on inaccurate reports made by espionage chief Allan Pinkerton may have accounted for this mistaken belief, although some commentators blame cowardice. His requests for reinforcements and extreme caution in attacking the Confederates during the Peninsula campaign led to a Union defeat. McClellan's failure to pursue Lee after the Battle of Antietam, even when ordered to do so, finally convinced Lincoln to relieve him of his command in November 1862.

George McClellan ran against Lincoln as the Democratic presidential candidate in 1864. He was elected governor of New Jersey in 1878 and served one term. McClellan died on October 29, 1885. He defended his military record in his autobiography, *McClellan's Own Story*, which was published in 1887.

WILMER McLEAN
(DATES UNKNOWN)

Although Wilmer McLean was not a soldier, he played an unusual supporting role in the Civil War. Early in the war, in June 1861, General Pierre G.T. Beauregard used McLean's home near Manassas Junction, Virginia, as Confederate headquarters during the First Battle of Bull Run. After an artillery shell ripped through his kitchen, McLean left Manassas and moved to a small town southwest of Richmond, to remove his family from the path of the war. Despite his intentions, McLean once again became involved in the war when, on April 9, 1865, Lee surrendered to Grant in the living room of his home at Appomattox Court House.

GEORGE GORDON MEADE
(1815-1872)

Union General George Gordon Meade was born in Cadiz, Spain, where his father was stationed as a naval agent. He served in the army for a year after his 1835 graduation from West Point and then worked as a civil engineer until 1842, when he returned to the army in the Corps of Topographical Engineers. He fought in the Mexican War under General Zachary Taylor and General Winfield Scott and remained in the army in various engineering positions until the start of the Civil War, when he was appointed to lead a brigade of Pennsylvania volunteers. Meade participated in the Peninsula campaign, the Second Battle of Bull Run, Antietam, Fredericksburg, and Chancellorsville. As he gained battlefield experience, he was rewarded with regular promotions and, in June 1863, Lincoln appointed him to succeed General Joseph Hooker as the commander of the Army of the Potomac. Only a few days later, Meade led the Union forces to a critical, but costly, victory at Gettysburg. After March 1864, when Grant was put in charge of all Union forces, he traveled with, and in many respects controlled, Meade's army. Although Meade was disliked by his troops because of his uncontrollable temper, he worked well with Grant for the remainder of the war. Meade remained in the army after the war and died on November 6, 1872, of pneumonia complicated by war wounds he had sustained 10 years earlier.

MEDAL OF HONOR

The Medal of Honor, also called the Congressional Medal of Honor, is the first and highest award for valor authorized by the United States government. It is comparable to England's Victoria Cross and to Germany's Iron Cross. Congress approved the Medal of Honor for enlisted sailors and marines in December 1861, and for enlisted army personnel in July 1862. Army officers were included in March 1863, but naval officers were not eligible for the award until 1915. The first recipients of the Medal of Honor were the six survivors of Andrews' Raid. Approximately 1,200 participants in the Civil War received the Medal of Honor. When the eligibility criteria for the decoration became more restrictive in 1916, a review board struck 911 recipients, a majority of them Civil War veterans, from the rolls, finding that they did not meet the revised standards.

MINIÉ BULLET

Called "minnie balls" by the troops, these rifle bullets changed the nature of warfare. Before French Army Captain Claude F. Minié designed these half-inch, hollow, lead bullets in 1848, loading rifles was too time-consuming to make their use practical on the battlefield. Minié balls were cheaper, easier to load, had a greater range, and reached their targets more accurately than earlier bullets. They also caused severe injury. Minié balls would shatter bones on impact, and soldiers hit in the head or abdomen by these heavy lead bullets would almost always die from their wounds.

MISSOURI COMPROMISE
(1820)

Before the westward expansion brought about by the Louisiana Purchase, slavery was limited to territories south of the Ohio River, under the Northwest Ordinance of 1787, and, farther to the east, to states south of the Mason-Dixon Line. The need for new boundaries became apparent in 1818 when Missouri sought admission to the Union as a slave state, even though most of Missouri was north of the Ohio River. The admission of Missouri also would throw off the balance between free and slave states in the United States Senate. When Maine sought statehood, the question of balance was resolved and Speaker of the House Henry Clay was able to work out the Missouri Compromise, which, in addition to admitting the two new states, nullified the Northwest Ordinance to establish the 36°30' parallel, or the southern border of Missouri, as the northernmost boundary for slavery in the remainder of the territory acquired by the Louisiana Purchase. The Missouri Compromise was the first in a series of legislative responses to the growing problem of slavery and implicitly empowered the federal government to decide the issue. It was repealed in 1854 by the Kansas-Nebraska Act.

MOBILE BAY, BATTLE OF
(AUGUST 5, 1864)

Mobile Bay, 30 miles south of Mobile, Alabama, was one of the Confederacy's last open ports during the Union blockade. Through this site, the South received much-needed provisions from Europe. The bay was defended by Admiral Franklin Buchanan's 470 Confederate naval personnel at Fort Morgan and aboard the South's largest ironclad ship, the CSS *Tennessee*, and three wooden gunboats. Admiral David G. Farragut led a Union force of 3,000 aboard a fleet of four ironclads and 14 wooden ships into the bay at 6:00 a.m. on August 5, 1864. Early in the battle, the Union ironclad, the USS *Tecumseh*, struck a mine and was destroyed. Heeding Farragut's legendary call to action, "Damn the torpedoes! Full speed ahead!" the Union fleet sailed through the mines into the bay. The heavily outnumbered Confederates continued to attack, but by 10:00 a.m. Mobile Bay was under Union control. Northern casualties numbered 319, including the 93 drowned and four taken prisoner when the

Tecumseh sank. Southern casualties numbered 312, with 280 captured, including Admiral Buchanan.

THE *MONITOR* VERSUS THE *MERRIMAC* (CSS *VIRGINIA*)
(MARCH 8, 1862)

When the North was forced to abandon the Norfolk Navy Yard in April 1861, the Confederates salvaged a scuttled steam frigate, the *Merrimac*, and covered its hull and deck with thick metal plates. Rechristened the CSS *Virginia* but generally referred to by its original name, the rebuilt *Merrimac* set off on its maiden voyage for Hampton Roads, Virginia, at the entrance of the Chesapeake Bay, which was a base for the Union blockade. The *Merrimac* sank two wooden ships and threatened the blockade on March 8, 1862. The USS *Monitor*, an iron ship nicknamed the "Yankee cheese box on a raft," arrived the next day. Although the two ironclads fought to a draw, leaving intact the Union

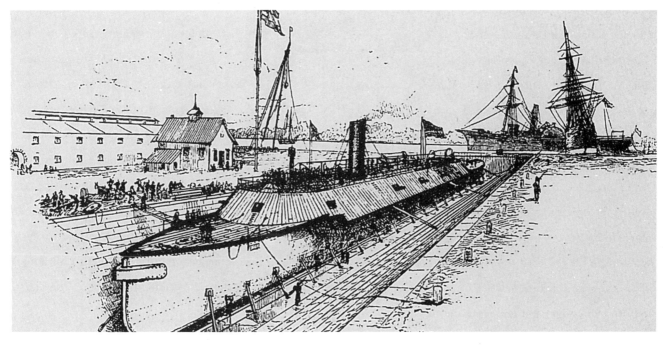

blockade at Hampton Roads, the battle demonstrated the importance of armored ships. The *Monitor-Merrimac* battle also is notable for being the first naval contest fought entirely under steam power.

MORGAN'S RAIDS
(JULY 1862-JULY 1863)

Confederate General John Hunt Morgan led daredevil cavalry raids into Union territory, going as far north as the border of Ohio and Pennsylvania. In July 1862, Morgan's Raiders left their base in Tennessee and traveled over 1,000 miles through Kentucky, capturing over 1,200 Union prisoners and destroying supply depots. Three months later, after capturing Lexington, Kentucky, Morgan's Raiders demolished federal rail and communications lines on their way back to Tennessee. During Morgan's "Christmas Raid" in December 1862, his 4,000-man brigade was responsible for the destruction of more than two million dollars worth of Union property and the capture of 1,900 Northern soldiers. In July 1863, Morgan disregarded orders to delay the Union advance on Chattanooga led by General Rosencrans. Instead, he invaded Ohio, leading his 2,500 troops on a 35-hour, 90-mile march, the longest continuous march of the war. By the time his reduced force of 2,000 men reached Ohio, they had taken 6,000 Union prisoners and destroyed 25 bridges and numerous railroads. Pursued

Brig Genl Jno Morgan

by 10,000 Union troops, about 120 raiders were killed and 700 were taken prisoner. Morgan and 300 men fled toward Pennsylvania but were captured and imprisoned in the Ohio State Penitentiary. Although Morgan escaped from prison in November 1863, his raiding days were over. He was killed in battle on September 3, 1864.

MOSBY'S RANGERS

Confederate Colonel John Singleton "Gray Ghost" Mosby served as a scout for Jeb Stuart during the Peninsula campaign, where he conceived the idea for, and participated in, Stuart's ride around McClellan in June 1862. He is best remembered, however, for commanding Mosby's Rangers, a corps of as many as 800 partisans, many of them civilians who were unwilling to enlist and soldiers convalescing from injuries or on leave. From December 1862 through April 1865, the rangers defended northern Virginia between the Potomac and Rappahannock Rivers, an area that came to be called "Mosby's Confederacy." Operating from no single base, they came together only when notified by Mosby. Known for their guerrilla tactics, they killed, wounded, or captured Union troops, destroyed rail lines, and seized horses, cattle, and supply wagons. Mosby's Rangers so successfully carried out their mission to sabotage the Union army in Virginia that some historians credit them with adding more than a year to the duration of the Confederacy.

NASHVILLE, BATTLE OF (DECEMBER 15-16, 1864)

Despite the devastating Confederate defeat at Franklin, Tennessee, two weeks earlier, General John Bell Hood was determined to retake Nashville, which had been occupied by Union forces for almost three years. He established a defensive line outside of the city with his 23,000 soldiers and prepared to face more than 55,000 Union troops under the command of General George Henry Thomas. Thomas attacked on December 15, 1864, forcing Hood's army to retreat and establish a new defensive position two miles away. When the attack was renewed during a severe rainstorm on December 16, the Northern victory was complete, and what was left of Hood's army fled to Mississippi. Hood resigned his command in January 1865.

THOMAS NAST (1840-1892)

Bavarian-born Thomas Nast was a cartoonist and war correspondent. His political cartoons, which first appeared in *Harper's Weekly* during the Civil War, helped to sway public opinion toward the Union. Perhaps best-known for his caricatures of William "Boss" Tweed during the Tammany Hall scandal in New York City in the 1870s, Nast also popularized the modern images of Santa Claus, the Democratic donkey, and the Republican elephant.

NATIVE AMERICANS IN THE CIVIL WAR

During the Civil War, approximately 3,600 Native Americans fought for the Union. One of the best known was Colonel Ely Parker, a Seneca who was an aide to General Ulysses S. Grant and was with him at Appomattox Court House. The Cherokee nation had divided loyalties arising from tribal reaction to a treaty that require the Cherokee to move from Georgia to the Oklahoma Territory. The Cherokees who disputed the treaty fought for the North, but the minority faction that agreed to the move fought for the Confederacy as the First Cherokee Mounted Rifles, under the command

Chippewa (Ojibwa) agent, Hole-In-The-Day.

of Chief Stand Watie. Throughout the war, federal troops in the Western territories fought a number of Native American tribes in an effort to control them and open the West for settlement by whites.

NEW ORLEANS, BATTLE OF (APRIL 25, 1862)

New Orleans, the largest city in the South, was the gateway to the Mississippi River and thus to the deep South. The mouth of the river was barricaded and defended by Forts Jackson and St. Philip, but the city was not heavily fortified. On April 18, Union Commander David Dixon Porter began a six-day bombardment of the forts that was more effective as a distraction than it was offensively. The assault enabled Captain David G. Farragut to sail his fleet through the Confederate barricade. Farragut's fleet won the ensuing naval battle and continued on its way upriver to New Orleans, which he captured with no further fighting on April 25, 1862. By May 1, New Orleans and southern Louisiana were occupied by the North, and they remained under Union control for the remainder of the war.

"NEWS WALKERS"

After a battle was over, some soldiers would walk around the camp, gathering and sharing news and information. These "news walkers" functioned as reporters, using the information they gleaned on their campfire rounds to try to gauge troop morale, determine how the day's fighting had gone, and figure out what was likely to happen next.

OLD CAPITOL PRISON

The Old Capitol Prison in Washington, D.C., was located in a run-down building that had temporarily replaced the United States Capitol after it was burned down by the British during the War of 1812, and later was used as a hotel. During the Civil War, the building served as a Union prison for deserters, spies, prisoners of war, and persons being detained for trial.

ORPHAN BRIGADE

The 1st Kentucky Brigade, 4,000 strong at the beginning of the war but with only 500 original members by the war's end, was known as the "Orphan Brigade" because it was a Confederate unit that came from a Union state. The brigade took part in such major battles as Shiloh, Vicksburg, Chickamauga, and the Atlanta campaign.

ELY SAMUEL PARKER
(1828-1895)

Born on a reservation in New York in 1828, Ely Samuel Parker, a Seneca originally named Donehogawa, was the highest-ranking Native American in the Union army. Parker studied law but was not admitted to the New York bar because he was not an American citizen. He earned a degree in civil engineering and took a position in Galena, Illinois, where he became friends with Ulysses S. Grant, who was then a shop clerk. Although he was denied a commission in the Union army at the beginning of the Civil War, Parker was commissioned a captain of engineers in 1863. He was promoted to lieutenant colonel when he became Grant's military secretary in August 1864. Parker transcribed the official copies of the terms of surrender when Lee surrendered to Grant at Appomattox Court House. During the proceedings, Lee commented that he was pleased that a "real American" was present, to which Parker replied, "Now we are all Americans." Ely Parker remained on Grant's staff after the war and in 1867 became his aide-de-camp and was promoted to brigadier general. President Grant appointed Parker Commissioner of Indian Affairs in 1869, making him the first Native American to hold that position. Accusations of corruption made by politicians critical of his defense of Native American rights were dismissed by congressional investigators, but he was forced to resign in 1871. Parker died in 1895.

PEACE DEMOCRATS

The Peace Democrats, a faction within the Democratic Party, opposed the Civil War and sought its immediate end. Prior to the 1864 election, the Democrats added a "peace plank" to their presidential platform. Even within the group, however, opinion was split on how to achieve this goal. One side, known as the Copperheads, argued for an end to the fighting even if it meant recognizing the Confederacy as an independent country. The other side advocated the reunification of the United States, which was the position taken by General George B. McClellan, the Democratic presidential candidate.

"PECULIAR INSTITUTION"

Southerners often resorted to euphemisms such as "peculiar institution" when discussing slavery. The term was popularized by states' rights advocate John Calhoun during his term as vice president under Andrew Jackson.

PENINSULA CAMPAIGN
(MARCH-AUGUST 1862)

Union General George B. McClellan transported 100,000 troops on 400 ships across the Chesapeake Bay to Fort Monroe, at the tip of the Virginia peninsula, in March 1862. His objective was the capture of Richmond, the Confederate capital. His men moved up the peninsula toward Yorktown and McClellan, believing Confederate General Joseph E. Johnston's forces to be much stronger than they actually were, exercised his

Valley to prevent the North from sending reinforcements to McClellan. Jackson's "foot cavalry" marched 350 miles toward Washington, D.C., winning four battles before being forced to retreat. Reinforced by Jackson's troops, Lee's Battles of the Seven Days in late June successfully defended Richmond and forced McClellan to retreat. His army moved on to reinforce General John Pope's forces for the Second Battle of Bull Run.

Union mortars at Yorktown during the Peninsula campaign.

usual caution before attacking. After launching an artillery attack, the Confederates abandoned Yorktown to the Union forces on May 3. Williamsburg followed, on May 5. By the end of May, the South had surrendered most of eastern Virginia, including the Norfolk Navy Yard. The Confederates attacked McClellan's troops on May 31 at the Battle of Fair Oaks (Seven Pines), slowing but not stopping the Northern advance. Johnston was replaced by the more aggressive General Robert E. Lee. To prepare for battle, Lee sent Confederate General Jeb Stuart on a "ride around McClellan," which garnered information about Union troop movement but also alerted McClellan to prepare for attack. In the meantime, from May 4 through June 9, Confederate General Stonewall Jackson created a diversion in the Shenandoah

PERRYVILLE, BATTLE OF (OCTOBER 8, 1862)

Hot, dry weather and unusual atmospheric conditions on October 8, 1862, played a major role in the Battle of Perryville, Kentucky's most important Civil War battle. The fighting began when Confederate troops discovered Union reconnaissance soldiers searching for water. Because the wind did not carry the din of the battlefield back to Union headquarters, General Don Carlos Buell was oblivious to the fighting for several hours. Thus, he did not deploy most of his troops until the battle was well under way. The Confederates, led by General Braxton Bragg, also fought with a reduced force, for parts of his army had remained near Frankfort. Both armies sustained heavy casualties—almost a quarter of the 16,000 Confederate soldiers, and more than a tenth of the 37,000 Union troops. Bragg retreated to Murfreesboro, Tennessee, and was censured by Jefferson Davis for los-

Confederate soldiers sit in a shallow trench awaiting action at Petersburg.

ing Kentucky. Although the outcome of the battle favored the North, Buell fared worse than Bragg; Lincoln censured him and stripped him of his command for failing to crush the retreating Confederates.

PERSONAL LIBERTY LAWS

In response to the Fugitive Slave Act that was part of the Compromise of 1850, the legislatures of 10 Northern states enacted personal liberty laws. These laws, which demonstrated the Northern interpretation of states' rights, prohibited state officials from assisting in the arrest of runaway slaves, precluded state prisons from holding them, and provided for jury trials for the fugitives.

PETERSBURG, SIEGE OF (JUNE 1864-MAY 1865)

In June 1864, Union General Ulysses S. Grant began moving the Army of the Potomac toward Petersburg, a major rail center south of Richmond. He realized that if he could capture Petersburg, Richmond would fall. Hoping for a quick victory, Grant was held off by a much smaller Confederate force led by General Pierre G.T. Beauregard. When General Robert E. Lee's Army of Northern Virginia arrived, the two sides settled in for what would turn out to be a 10-month siege. The Battle of the Crater, on July 30, was perhaps the most original, if unsuccessful, episode of the war; a Union regiment filled a 500-foot tunnel with explosives to rout the Confederate defense,

The mortar known as "The Dictator" sits on the railroad at Petersburg.

but the assault was a fiasco for the North. Over the course of the Petersburg campaign, boredom, extreme temperatures, hunger, and disease proved to be as treacherous to the soldiers in the trenches, especially the ill-equipped Confederates, as the fighting was. The siege of Petersburg continued until the end of the war. Petersburg was occupied by the North on April 2, 1865, and Richmond fell on April 3.

PICKETT'S CHARGE
(JULY 3, 1863)

On the third day of the Battle of Gettysburg, July 3, 1863, Confederate General Robert E. Lee ordered General James Longstreet to breach the Union stronghold at Cemetery Ridge. After hours of artillery bombardment, the Confederates

believed that they had overpowered the enemy and sent 14,000 soldiers, under the supervision of Confederate General George Edward Pickett, across an open field and up the ridge. The Union troops, who had earlier stopped fighting to save on ammunition, opened fire on the precisely arranged columns of Confederates. As the Southerners continued to advance, the fighting changed to hand-to-hand combat. Pickett's Charge lasted for less than an hour, but over half of his men were killed. The Battle of Gettysburg had been lost, and the Confederate army headed back to Virginia, never to regain its former strength.

ALLAN PINKERTON
(1819-1884)

Glasgow-born Allan Pinkerton emigrated to the United States in 1842. He was an abolitionist, and his home in Chicago was a station on the Underground Railroad. Pinkerton established a detective agency in 1850. In 1861, he warned President-elect Abraham Lincoln of an alleged assassination plot. At the start of the Civil War, Lincoln asked Pinkerton to organize a federal secret service. Before going off to join

General George B. McClellan, he exposed the Confederate espionage operations run by Rose O'Neal Greenhow. Using the name "Major E.J. Allen," Pinkerton provided McClellan with information on Confederate troop strength, but the information was not accurate. In fact, his overestimation of the size of opposing forces may have contributed to McClellan's requests for reinforcements and hesitation to take action during the Peninsula campaign. When McClellan was removed from command, Pinkerton returned to his private investigation work in Chicago.

JOHN POPE (1822-1892)

An 1842 graduate of West Point, Union General John Pope served in the West as an engineer until he joined the Union army. After capturing New Madrid and Corinth, Missouri, in March 1862, which played a critical role opening the Mississippi River to Union navigation, Lincoln appointed him to replace the overly cautious General George B. McClellan. Pope commanded the Union army at the Second Battle of Bull Run in late August 1862 but was outmaneuvered by Confederate General Robert E. Lee. Lincoln removed Pope from his command and reinstated McClellan immediately after the battle. Pope spent the remainder of the war in the Northwest, dealing with Native American affairs.

POPULAR SOVEREIGNTY

According to the doctrine of popular sovereignty, it was up the people of a territory, not Congress, to decide whether to permit slavery in the territory. Popularized by Stephen A. Douglas, the doctrine was the basis for the Kansas-Nebraska Act of 1854. The ensuing border wars, however, demonstrated that popular sovereignty was not a feasible solution to the problem of slavery.

DAVID DIXON PORTER
(1813-1891)

David Dixon Porter, a member of a renowned American naval family, fought pirates in the West Indies when he was 10 years old and was a midshipman in the Mexican Navy by the time he was 14 years old. Two years later, he joined the United States navy. From 1846 through 1848, he participated in every naval engagement of the Mexican War. Active throughout the Civil War, Porter played a major role in the Battle of New Orleans in April 1862, where he directed the bombardment of Forts Jackson and St. Philip that enabled Captain David Farragut, his foster brother, to sail into the harbor and crush the Confederate fleet. In January 1863, Porter opened the Mississippi River to Union navigation when he combined forces with General William Tecumseh Sherman to capture the Arkansas Post (Fort Hindman). He was promoted to rear admiral for his service at Vicksburg and was appointed to command the North Atlantic Blockading Squadron in 1864. On January 14, 1865, Porter participated in the capture the Confederacy's last open East Coast port, Fort Fisher, North Carolina. David Dixon Porter was the superintendent of the United States Naval Academy from 1865 through 1869. He was promoted to vice admiral in 1866 and Admiral of the Navy in 1870, succeeding Farragut.

FITZ-JOHN PORTER

(1822-1901)

Union General Fitz-John Porter, a cousin of Admiral David Dixon Porter, broke with the naval tradition of his family and graduated from West Point in 1845. Prior to the Civil War, he served with Generals Zachary Taylor and Winfield Scott in the Mexican War, taught at West Point, and was involved in the Mormon Expedition to Utah in 1857. Porter participated in many battles during the war, including the Peninsula campaign and Antietam, but he is best remembered because General John Pope brought charges against him for disloyalty, misconduct, and refusing to obey an order to attack Confederate General Stonewall Jackson's corps during the Second Battle of Bull Run in August 1862. Found guilty by a court martial in January 1863, he was dismissed from the army. After years of trying to prove his innocence, Porter's case was reopened in 1879; the review board ruled in his favor, but he was not reappointed to the army until 1886, when he was immediately put on the retired list.

Fitz-John Porter and his staff in June, 1862.

"QUAKER GUNS"

Early in the war, Confederate forces used logs painted to resemble cannons to trick Union scouts into believing that they were more heavily armed than they actually were. The effective use of these "Quaker guns" contributed to Union General George McClellan's delay in attacking Yorktown, Virginia, during the Peninsula campaign in the spring of 1862.

WILLIAM CLARK QUANTRILL

(1837-1865)

The notorious William Clark Quantrill, also known as Charley Hart, led brutal guerrilla raids in Kansas and Missouri. Known as "bushwhackers," Quantrill and his Confederate followers terrorized civilians and Union troops more from their love of mayhem and looting than out of any deep political convictions. In August 1862, Quantrill and his men captured Independence, Missouri, for which he was awarded a commission as a captain in the Confederate army. On August 21, 1863, his 400-member command, which included Frank and Jesse James and the Younger brothers, burned the anti-slavery town of Lawrence, Kansas, killing 150 boys and men and demolishing one and a half million dollars worth of property. Late in the war, Quantrill headed east to assassinate President Lincoln. During a raid in Kentucky, he was mortally wounded by federal soldiers. He died in May 1865.

RADICAL REPUBLICANS

During the Civil War, the Republican Party was divided between those sought gradual emancipation and favored non-punitive treatment of the post-war South and a more extreme faction, that wanted immediate emancipation and were determined to destroy the existing economic and political structure of the South. These extremists, known as the Radical Republicans, made up only about a third of the party but they became its dominant voice during the war and its aftermath. Although Lincoln was a moderate, his treasury secretary, Salmon P. Chase, and his secretary of war, Edwin M. Stanton, were Radical Republicans. Congressional leadership included Senator Charles Sumner, Senator Benjamin Wade, Representative Thaddeus Stevens, and Representative Henry Davis. Radical Republicans in Congress created the Joint Committee on the Conduct of the War, which targeted Union generals reputed to be lenient toward the South.

Reconstruction was the area of greatest difference between the moderates and the Radical Republicans. Rather than the gradual reunification envisioned by the moderates, the Radical Republicans, who gained control of Reconstruction after Lincoln's assassination, worked to create a new social order in the South based on equal opportunity for all people. The Radical Republicans remained in power until the end of Grant's second administration, in 1876, when they were brought down by a recession and by charges of corruption.

"REBEL YELL"

Along with their more traditional arsenal of weapons, Confederate troops used a high-pitched, piercing battle cry known as the "Rebel Yell." This shrieking wail, which may have developed from the Southern fox hunters' cry, was as unnerving to Union soldiers as it was exhilarating to the charging Confederates.

RECONSTRUCTION (1865-1877)

Known in the South as the "Tragic Era," Reconstruction was the period after the Civil War during which the North attempted to rebuild the South politically, socially, and economically. As early as October 8, 1863, Lincoln had issued a Proclamation of Amnesty and Reconstruction, which provided for a full pardon for anyone who pledged to accept abolition and who took a loyalty oath reaffirming allegiance to the Union. Under this non-punitive approach to bringing the Southern states back into the Union, if 10 percent of a state's population

THE RADICAL CONVENTION
In Philadelphia, September 3d, 1866.
GEARY The CANDIDATE for GOVERNOR WAS IN THE PROCESSION
EVERY RADICAL CANDIDATE
For UNITED STATES SENATOR took part.
White Men & Women
ARE YOU READY FOR THIS?

met these terms, the state could be represented in Congress. Additionally, the Southern states were permitted to adapt gradually to a free economy before slavery was completely abolished, and high-ranking members of the Confederate military remained subject to prosecution. President Andrew Johnson's attempts to continue Lincoln's program almost led to his removal by the Radical Republican-controlled Congress.

When Reconstruction came under legislative rather than executive jurisdiction, the Radical Republicans enacted a much more stringent policy that included immediate abolition, civil rights for blacks, and harsh sanctions against former Confederates. Under the Reconstruction Act of 1867, the South was divided into five military districts occupied by Union troops, Southerners were required to take a loyalty oath, and Confederate leaders were restricted from holding public office. During Reconstruction, three amendments were added to the United States Constitution. The Thirteenth Amendment, adopted in 1865, outlawed slavery. The Fourteenth Amendment, passed in 1868, granted citizenship to freed slaves and provided for equal protection of the laws. The Fifteenth Amendment, ratified in 1870, granted blacks the right to vote. Although all of the former Confederate states had returned to the Union by 1870, the federal military occupation did not completely cease until 1877. Southern resentment of the changes brought by Reconstruction, especially in terms of voting and equal rights for African-Americans, led to the formation of the Ku Klux Klan during this period.

Republican Candidates in 1856 presidential election, Frémont and Dayton.

REPUBLICAN PARTY

Opposition to the Kansas-Nebraska Act of 1854 led to the formation of a new, antislavery political party. The Republican Party's first presidential nominee, in 1856, was John Frémont. The second Republican to run for president, Abraham Lincoln, won the 1860 election by a majority of electoral votes, although he received only 40 percent of the popular vote. In 1864, when the Republicans formed a coalition with the War Democrats and called themselves the National Union Party, Lincoln's win was more decisive. The Republican Party split into three factions during the war—conservatives, moderates, and Radical Republicans—each with a different approach to abolition and Reconstruction, ranging from gradual to immediate emancipation and from lenient to punitive treatment of the former Confederate states. The Radical Republicans, the most extreme group, gained control of the party with the impeachment of President Andrew Johnson, and they remained the dominant Republican force until the moderate Rutherford B. Hayes was elected president in 1876.

RICHMOND, VIRGINIA

Located only 100 miles from Washington, D.C., Richmond, Virginia, was the capital of the Confederacy. The most important manufacturing center in the South, Richmond was a major producer of iron, flour and cornmeal, and tobacco. It also housed Chimborazo, the largest hospital in the South, as well as Belle Island and Libby military prisons. In response to the rampant inflation and shortages of essential goods caused by the war, almost 1,000 women ransacked shops and bakeries during the Richmond Bread Riot of April 1863, until Jefferson Davis intervened in the protest. Richmond was a major target of the Union throughout the war, but it was not captured until April 2, 1865, after the fall of Petersburg.

EDMUND RUFFIN (1794-1865)

Sixty-five years old when the Civil War started, Edmund Ruffin, a Southern aristocrat, agriculturalist, and passionate secessionist, left his native Virginia for South Carolina because of what he viewed as Virginia's hesitation in leaving the Union. Ruffin allegedly fired the first shot of the war at Fort Sumter on April 12, 1861; it is more likely that his shot was symbolic and that the shooting had already begun. He also claimed to have fired the cannon that started the Union retreat at First Bull Run. Unable to bear the Confederacy's loss and unwilling to live under a Yankee government, Ruffin committed suicide on June 17, 1865.

SANITARY COMMISSION

When the Civil War began, women across the country began to organize military relief organizations to provide health and medical services not available from the government. These groups were consolidated when Lincoln authorized the creation of the United States Sanitary Commission in June 1861. Within two years, the Sanitary Commission had 500 employees, most of whom were men, and thousands of volunteers, most of whom were women, in 7,000 local chapters. Two of the most active women, Mary Livermore, who became a national director in December 1862, and Jane Hoge, organized hundreds of groups in the Midwest and went on speaking tours to garner funds and support for the commission. One of their most successful fundraising ideas was to hold carnivals with food, entertainment, games, and exhibitions. The first Sanitary Fair, held in Chicago for two weeks in the autumn of 1863, included an auction of the original draft of the Emancipation Proclamation and brought in as much as $300,000; similar fairs held in Philadelphia and New York each raised over one million dollars for the cause. Over the course of the war, the Sanitary Commission successfully lobbied for reforms in the Army Medical Bureau and spent over 20 million dollars to improve the conditions in military camps and hospitals by providing medical supplies, health care workers, food, clothing, and expert advice and assistance on nutrition and disease prevention.

SCALAWAGS

Scalawags, or "no good scoundrels," was the pejorative term used for white Southern Republicans during Reconstruction. Considered traitors by those who retained their loyalty to the Confederacy, the scalawags encompassed war veterans, including former Confederate General James Longstreet, reformers, entrepreneurs, and struggling farmers. Scalawags worked with the Northern carpetbaggers as well as with the Republican administration in Washington, believing that their cooperation would prove to be politically and economically advantageous.

WINFIELD SCOTT
(1 7 8 6 - 1 8 6 6)

Union General Winfield "Old Fuss and Feathers" Scott, a Virginian who rejected the Confederacy, had been the general-in-chief of the United States army since 1841. He served in the army during the War of 1812, the Black Hawk War, and the Mexican War, where he was responsible for winning many critical battles; a national hero, Scott was the Whig candidate for President in 1852. When the Civil War began, Scott proposed the Anaconda Plan, a naval blockade of the Mississippi River that would give the Union more time to ready its armed forces for prolonged fighting. Early Northern losses convinced Lincoln to accept Scott's resignation in November 1861. Succeeded as general-in-chief by his field commander, George B. McClellan, Scott died in 1866, after seeing his predictions for the duration of the war confirmed and

knowing that major aspects of his blockade plan had indeed contributed to the Union victory.

SECESSION

Throughout the 1800s, the balance of economic and political power in the United States was shifting to the more populous, industrialized North and away from the agrarian South. When Lincoln won the 1860 presidential election, Southerners feared that slavery, which was essential to maintain the Southern way of life, would be abolished. South Carolina seceded from the Union on December 20, 1860. Six other states soon followed: Mississippi (January 9, 1861), Florida (January 10), Alabama (January 11), Georgia (January 19), Louisiana (January 26), and Texas (February 1). State delegates convened in Montgomery, Alabama, on February 4, 1861; on February 8, they adopted a provisional constitution that established the Confederate States of America, and on February 9 they elected a president, Jefferson Davis, and a vice president, Alexander Stephens. Two months later, following the fall of Fort Sumter, four additional states joined the Confederacy: Virginia (April 17), Arkansas (May 6), North Carolina (May 20), and Tennessee (June 8). Kentucky and Missouri had Confederate and Union governments throughout the war. West Virginia broke away from Virginia on August 20, 1862, and became a state on June 20, 1863. The Confederacy officially was dissolved when Lee surrendered to Grant at Appomattox Court House on April 9, 1865, and the states that had broken away rejoined the Union during Reconstruction.

WILLIAM HENRY SEWARD

(1801-1872)

William Henry Seward first entered politics when he was elected on the Whig ticket to the New York legislature in 1830. He served one term as governor of New York, from 1838 until 1842, and was elected to the United States Senate in 1849, where he was a vocal opponent of slavery. An early member of the Republican Party, Seward unsuccessfully sought its presidential nominations in 1856 and 1860. As Lincoln's secretary of state, Seward avoided war with Britain by negotiating the settlement of the *Trent* Affair. Later, despite his own abolitionist beliefs, he advised Lincoln to wait to issue the Emancipation Proclamation until the Union had won some significant military battles. One of the targets of the Lincoln assassination conspirators, Seward was attacked in his home and severely injured on April 14, 1865. When he recovered, he remained in the cabinet as Johnson's secretary of state, where his most notable accomplishment was the purchase of Alaska, known by his detractors as "Seward's Folly" and "Seward's Icebox," from Russia in 1867.

ROBERT GOULD SHAW

(1837-1863)

Although the soldiers and the noncommissioned officers in the 54th Massachusetts Regiment, the first African-American regiment in the Union army, were black, its commanding officers were white. The commander of the unit was Colonel Robert Gould Shaw, the Boston-bred son of wealthy abolitionists. Killed during the regiment's initial battle, an assault on Fort Wagner in

Charleston, South Carolina, Shaw was buried on the battlefield in a trench grave with his fallen soldiers.

Philip Sheridan at his tent at Lighthouse Point, Virginia in 1864.

PHILIP HENRY SHERIDAN

(1831-1888)

Union General Philip Henry "Little Phil" Sheridan began his military career inauspiciously, when he was suspended for a year from West Point for attacking another cadet. He returned to graduate in 1853 and served in Texas and the Northwest prior to the outbreak of the Civil War. Initially a quartermaster, or supply officer, Sheridan distinguished himself as a commander at the Battles of Perryville, in October 1862, and Stones River, on December 31, 1862, where his 5,000 troops withstood more than twice as many Confederates and paved the way for a Union victory. In 1863, he took part in the Battles of Winchester, Chicamauga, and Chattanooga, where he stormed Missionary Ridge, nearly captured several Confederate generals, including Braxton Bragg, and led the only unit that pursued the retreating Southerners. In early May 1864, Sheridan fought in the Battles of the Wilderness and Spotsylvania Court House, and from May 9 through 24, he conducted "Sheridan's Richmond Raid," during which Confederate General Jeb Stuart was mortally wounded at the Battle of Yellow Tavern on May 11. By the time Sheridan's raid was completed, he had ridden around Lee's army, confiscated innumerable supplies, and destroyed miles of Confederate transportation and communications lines.

In August 1864, Sheridan assumed command of all Union forces in the Shenandoah Valley. Sheridan's Shenandoah Valley campaign, which lasted almost until the end of the war, demolished Confederate General Jubal Early's forces and devastated the countryside. Following the "scorched earth" policy advocated by General William T. Sherman, his commander, Sheridan burned crops, wrecked property, and appropriated livestock and provisions throughout the valley, which was known as the "breadbasket of the Confederacy." In April 1865, Sheridan joined forces with Grant for the final assaults on Confederate General Robert E. Lee's army, and he was present at Appomattox Court House for Lee's surrender.

During Reconstruction, Sheridan commanded the Military Division of the Mississippi, but his harsh policies led to his removal after only six months. He became a noted general in the West and was an observer with the German Army during the Franco-Prussian War in the early 1870s. In 1884, Sheridan became general-in-chief of the United States Army, following Sherman's retirement.

WILLIAM TECUMSEH SHERMAN
(1820-1891)

Because of his conviction that "the crueler [a war] is, the sooner it will be over," which translated into his practice of "total war"—destroying property and undermining the day-to-day lives of civilians to bring about a more rapid resolution to the war with fewer casualties—many historians view Union General William Tecumseh Sherman as the first person to practice modern warfare techniques. An 1840 graduate of West Point, Sherman fought in the Second Seminole War and in the Mexican War. He resigned his commission in 1853 and became a businessman and a lawyer. In 1859, he became the superintendent of the military school that later became Louisiana State University at Baton Rouge.

At the beginning of the Civil War, Sherman declined the offer of a commission in the Confederate army and briefly returned to business. He was appointed a colonel in the Union army and in August 1861, after the First Battle of Bull Run, was promoted to brigadier general. Assuming command of Union forces in Kentucky after General Robert Anderson became ill, Sherman was rumored to be mentally unstable because of his criticism of an order to invade eastern Tennessee, as well as a dispute with the press. He was removed from his command and sent to Missouri. In April 1862, Sherman was wounded early in the Battle of Shiloh but refused to leave the battlefield. His bravery at Shiloh and at Corinth, Mississippi, led to another promotion and a lifelong friendship with his commander, General Ulysses S. Grant. Sherman participated in Grant's Vicksburg campaign in July 1863, and in the Chattanooga campaign, under General William S. Rosencrans, in November. When Grant was promoted to general-in-chief, Sherman took over the Western command and, in April 1864, he embarked on his Atlanta and Carolinas campaigns. After capturing and setting fire to Atlanta, Sherman led his troops on a "March to the Sea," devastating the Georgia countryside as they moved toward Savannah. The march, and the destruction, continued through the Carolinas until April 14, 1865, when Confederate General Joseph E. Johnston requested surrender terms at Durham Station, North Carolina. Sherman initially offered uncharacteristically lenient terms, until ordered by President Johnson to renegotiate; Johnston officially surrendered to Sherman on April 26.

Sherman continued to receive promotions after the war, culminating in his appointment as general-in-chief after Grant was elected president, a position he held from 1869 until late 1883. He published his *Memoirs* in 1875. Sought as a presidential candidate by both parties, Sherman's response to the Republicans in 1884 is one of the most famous lines in American history: "I will not accept if nominated and will not serve if elected." Sherman retired from the army on February 8, 1884. He died on February 14, 1891.

SHERMAN'S MARCH TO THE SEA (NOVEMBER 15– DECEMBER 21, 1864)

Leaving Atlanta burning in their wake, 62,000 soldiers commanded by Union General William T.

Grant's last line at Shiloh.

Sherman began to advance across Georgia on November 15, 1864. Opposed, but not hampered, by 13,000 Confederate troops, Sherman was determined to destroy Confederate civilian morale and to cut off all communications lines and supplies needed to sustain Robert E. Lee's army. Although officially under orders to avoid excessive looting and plunder, Sherman's men took what they wanted—the autumn harvest, livestock, munitions—and vandalized or destroyed houses, farms, and everything else in their path. As the march progressed, their ranks also included as many as 25,000 former slaves, Union and Confederate army deserters, and other "bummers," or foragers. Milledgeville, the state capital, fell on November 23. By December 10, when the marchers reached Savannah, they had traveled almost 300 miles and had caused over $100 million worth of damage. Confederate defenses abandoned the city on December 21, and Sherman offered it to Lincoln as a "Christmas gift." He then began his final, and even more brutal, assault on the birthplace of the Confederacy, the Carolinas campaign.

SHILOH
(PITTSBURG LANDING),
BATTLE OF
(APRIL 6-7, 1862)

Ironically, the Battle of Shiloh took its name from a Methodist church near the battlefield whose name came from the Hebrew term for "place of peace." In the North, it originally was referred to as the Battle of Pittsburg Landing, for the small Tennessee town where it took place. Union General Ulysses S. Grant's troops gathered near the Mississippi border in early spring 1862, waiting for reinforcement from General Don Carlos Buell before the combined forces would move south toward Corinth, an important Confederate rail center. On April 6, before Buell arrived, Confederate

Generals Albert Sidney Johnston and Pierre G.T. Beauregard executed a surprise attack. The South succeeded in overcoming Grant's defense of a strategic site known as "the Hornet's Nest" and forced the Union troops to retreat to Pittsburg Landing. This Confederate victory was mitigated when Johnston was killed in battle. By the next morning, Buell's reinforcements arrived. With an army twice the size of the Southern force, the Union forced Beauregard to retreat to Corinth.

Historians consider Shiloh a "soldier's battle," one that relied on the bravery of its soldiers rather than the leadership of its generals. Strategically, the battle was a draw. However, the North was victorious because it held its ground and caused the South to abandon a large area of Tennessee. Almost 3,500 soldiers died, and total casualties numbered 13,047 for the Union and 10,694

for the Confederates, making Shiloh the bloodiest battle of the war up to that time.

SLAVERY

Dutch traders brought the first African slaves to Jamestown, Virginia, in 1619. By the start of the Civil War, there were over four million slaves in the South, making up one-third of its population. Slaves were considered necessary because of the labor-intensive production requirements of cotton, tobacco, and rice, the three major crops that sustained the Southern agrarian economy; racial superiority was another argument used in favor of slavery. Although the conditions under which slaves lived varied, their legal status did not. Slaves had no legal rights. They were their owners' property and

Freed slaves at temporary housing in Alexandria, Virginia circa 1863.

were treated as chattel, not as human beings. Slaves could not marry or own property. They could not bring lawsuits or testify in court. They could not prevent the break-up of their families if their owners decided to sell them.

A unified abolitionist movement began with the founding of the American Anti-Slavery Society in 1833, and the formation of the Underground Railroad. Slavery entered the political arena with the debate over statehood for Missouri, which resulted in the Missouri Compromise of 1820. The debate over slavery intensified in the 1850s, as evidenced by the passage of the Fugitive Slave Act and the Kansas-Nebraska Act, the formation of the Republican Party, the Supreme Court's *Dred Scott* decision, the Lincoln-Douglas debates, and John Brown's Raid. Lincoln's

election to the presidency in 1860 sparked secession and the Civil War. Although the reunification of the country was Lincoln's immediate goal, slavery moved to the forefront when he issued the Emancipation Proclamation on January 1, 1863, which freed the slaves living in the Confederacy. Complete abolition was achieved in 1865, with the ratification of the Thirteenth Amendment to the United States Constitution.

ROBERT SMALLS
(1839-1915)

As a slave, Robert Smalls was hired out by his master to pilot the *Planter*, a Confederate supply boat. On May 13, 1862, after the captain went ashore, Smalls and seven black crew members

took charge. Wearing the captain's hat and coat, Smalls saluted and sailed past the Confederate defenses in Charleston Harbor, stopping long enough to pick up family members from the dock. He then surrendered the boat and its supplies, along with information about Charleston's defenses, to a Union blockade ship outside the harbor. Smalls was rewarded with a Union appointment as captain of the Planter, which he commanded for the rest of the war.

During Reconstruction, Smalls entered politics. He was a state legislator in South Carolina from 1868 through 1875 and represented South Carolina in Congress from 1875 to 1879, and again from 1882 to 1887.

SPOTSYLVANIA, BATTLE OF
(MAY 7-19, 1864)

Immediately after the Battle of the Wilderness, Union General Ulysses S. Grant continued his relentless pursuit of Confederate General Robert E. Lee's army in a series of Northern attacks and Southern counterattacks around Spotsylvania Court House, 40 miles north of Richmond. The fighting was brutal; an oak tree almost two feet in diameter was felled by the bullets fired during one of the most vicious skirmishes, a 20-hour battle on May 12 at the "Bloody Angle," also known as "The Salient." Union casualties during the Battle of Spotsylvania exceeded 17,500 and Confederate casualties reached 10,000. Despite their heavy losses, however, neither side could claim victory, and Grant and Lee moved on to their next confrontation, at Cold Harbor.

EDWIN MCMASTERS STANTON
(1814-1869)

Ohio-born Edwin McMasters Stanton was appointed attorney-general by President James Buchanan in 1860. After Lincoln's election, he resumed his law practice until early 1862, when Lincoln appointed him to replace Secretary of War Simon Cameron. An outspoken Radical Republican whose views often clashed with Lincoln's, Stanton nevertheless was an effective war secretary, and he retained his cabinet post when President Andrew Johnson took office. Stanton's opposition to Johnson's Reconstruction policies led Johnson to request his resignation. He refused to leave office and Johnson suspended him, appointing Ulysses S. Grant as his replacement. Stanton was restored to his position by Congress, which began impeachment proceedings against Johnson, alleging that he had abused his presidential power. Johnson was acquitted and, in May 1868, Stanton resigned from the cabinet and returned once again to his private law practice. Nominated to the Supreme Court by President Ulysses S. Grant, Stanton died on December 24, 1869, four days after his appointment was confirmed.

STAR OF THE WEST

The *Star of the West*, an unarmed ship carrying Union troops and supplies for Fort Sumter, was fired on when it arrived in Charleston Harbor on January 9, 1861, and forced to return to New York with its cargo intact. Thus, the first shots of the Civil War actually were fired three months before Fort Sumter fell to the Confederates.

STATES' RIGHTS

As soon as the United State Constitution was ratified in 1787, different interpretations arose concerning the relationship between the "necessary and proper" rights of the federal government and those reserved to the states. Slavery became a states' rights issue in the 1820s, with the westward expansion of the country. The most radical version of states' rights, however, was the nullification doctrine espoused by Senator John Calhoun that was adopted by his home state of South Carolina in 1832. Under this theory, a state could declare illegal federal laws that invaded its rights within its own borders. Secession was the result of carrying Calhoun's nullification doctrine to its logical extreme.

ALEXANDER HAMILTON STEPHENS
(1812-1883)

Confederate Vice President Alexander Hamilton Stephens was born in Georgia and graduated at the top of his class at the University of Georgia in 1832. Admitted to the bar in 1834, Stephens was elected to the Georgia legislature in 1836 and to the United States House of Representatives in 1843. Although he was an avid supporter of slavery and states' rights, he did not advocate secession. When Georgia seceded in January 1861, however, he transferred his loyalty to the Confederacy, and he was elected vice president the next month. Stephens led the legislative and executive opposition when President Jefferson Davis proposed such nationalistic policies as imposing a draft, levying taxes, and suspending *habeas corpus*. Stephens did not relinquish his hope for peace until February 1865, when he participated in the abortive Hampton Roads Conference.

When the war ended, Stephens was imprisoned until October 1865 at Fort Warren, in Boston. He then returned to Georgia and was elected to the United States Senate in 1866, but he was prohibited from serving his term because of a Reconstruction-era ban on former Confederates holding public office. Stephens turned to writing and published *A Constitutional View of the Late War Between the States* and other books before becoming the editor of *The Atlanta Southern Sun* in 1871. Elected to Congress in 1872, after the Confederate ban had been lifted, he served in the House of Representatives until 1882, when he was elected governor of Georgia. Stephens died several months later.

THADDEUS STEVENS
(1792-1868)

Thaddeus Stevens, the leader of the Radical Republicans in Congress during Reconstruction, was born in Vermont but moved to Gettysburg, Pennsylvania in 1816, where he established a law practice. During this period, he first became aware of slavery, and he often provided free legal services to fugitive slaves. Stevens served in the Pennsylvania legislature before being elected as a Whig to the United States House of Representatives in 1848. His strong abolitionist views led him the Republican Party, and he became a leader of its

Radical Republican offshoot. As chair of the Ways and Means Committee, Stevens was influential in passing legislation to support the Union war effort. After the war, as chair of the Joint Committee on Reconstruction, Stevens played a critical role in the creation of the Freedmen's Bureau and in the enactment of the Civil Rights Act of 1867. He also spearheaded the impeachment proceedings brought against President Andrew Johnson in February 1868. Thaddeus Stevens died on August 11, 1868.

STONES RIVER (MURFREESBORO), BATTLE OF (DECEMBER 31, 1862- JANUARY 2, 1863)

After the Battle of Perryville in October 1862, Confederate General Braxton Bragg retreated to Murfreesboro, Tennessee. Union General William S. Rosencrans moved his army south from Nashville toward the Confederate encampment near Stones River. By the end of December, both generals came up with the same plan, to attack the opposition's right flank. Bragg made the first move, forcing Rosencrans into a defensive position. After several days of fighting, each side had lost almost a third of its soldiers, the highest casualty rate of the war. Tactically, the South had won, but Bragg inexplicably retreated, allowing Rosencrans to take Murfreesboro and claim the victory.

HARRIET BEECHER STOWE
(1811-1896)

An overnight sensation for *Uncle Tom's Cabin*, her antislavery novel, Abraham Lincoln jokingly referred to Harriet Beecher Stowe as "the little lady who caused the Civil War." Born in Connecticut, she moved to Cincinnati, Ohio, when she was 21 years old, where her father was the president of Lane Theological Seminary. She married Calvin Stowe, a member of the Lane faculty, in 1836. In 1850, the Stowes moved to Maine, where she completed *Uncle Tom's Cabin* in 1852. Although her knowledge of slavery was second-hand, based on abolitionist pamphlets and her imagination, her story was sufficiently realistic to galvanize passions on both sides of the escalating debate over slavery and to make her name hated in the South. Four years later, she wrote another novel that dealt with slavery, *Dred, A Tale of the Great Dismal Swamp*. For the most part, her later novels and short stories concerned the effects of Puritanism on daily life in New England. In 1870, however, Harriet Beecher Stowe found herself in the midst of another literary controversy when she published *Lady Byron Vindicated*, which was considered to be one of the most scandalous books of the time.

JAMES EWELL BROWN "JEB" STUART
(1833-1864)

Called "the eyes and ears of my army" by Robert E. Lee, Confederate General James Ewell Brown "Jeb" Stuart was a study in contrasts, a deeply religious man with a vain, wild side to his personality. Born in Virginia in 1833, Stuart was an 1854 West Point graduate who served on the Western frontier and in Kansas during the border wars. In 1859, he volunteered for duty on Lee's staff during John Brown's raid on Harpers Ferry. When Virginia seceded in 1861, Stuart joined the Confederate army. Although his performance at the First Battle of Bull Run earned him a promotion to brigadier general, his flair for risky missions first became apparent during the Peninsula campaign in June 1862. Instead of the limited scouting assignment Lee had ordered, Stuart led his 1,000 cavalry troops on a bold 150-mile "ride around McClellan," destroying Union supplies and capturing dozens of prisoners while gathering critical information about the opposing forces. Promoted to major general in command of Lee's cavalry in July, he went on to fight at Second Bull Run and Antietam; it was Jeb Stuart who informed Lee that Special Order No. 191, the Confederate battle plan, had been discovered by Union soldiers. Stuart went on to Chambersburg, Pennsylvania, where he undertook his second "ride around McClellan." He fought at Fredericksburg and took command of Jackson's units at Chancellorsville in May 1863, after Jackson was mortally wounded. On June 9, Stuart fought in the largest cavalry battle in American history, the Battle of Brandy Station, Virginia. Stuart's independence backfired during a scouting mission to learn about Union troop deployment prior to the Battle of Gettysburg and contributed to the Confederate defeat, but he redeemed himself during the Wilderness campaign and the Battle of Spotsylvania in 1864. Jeb Stuart died on May 12, 1864, from a wound he had sustained the previous day during the Battle of Yellow Tavern, one of the skirmishes in Sheridan's Richmond Raid.

SUBMARINES

Looking for a way to break the Union's naval blockades, the South turned to submarine warfare. In 1861, the Confederates had built the CSS *Pioneer*, but they destroyed it when New Orleans was captured, to keep it out of Northern hands. The CSS *Hunley* was their next effort. Built in 1863, the cigar-shaped, iron, eight-man submarine carried a torpedo filled with 90 pounds of powder. General Pierre G.T. Beauregard put the *Hunley* into service in Charleston on February 17, 1864, against the USS *Housatonic*. The submarine quickly sank the Union sloop, but it became entangled in the boat's rigging and sank along with it. The CSS *St. Patrick* was the South's final attempt at submarine warfare, at Mobile, Alabama, in 1865. Its torpedo failed and the submarine was returned to port.

The Union's only submarine was the USS *Alligator*. Powered by manually operated oars, it sank off the coast of Cape Hatteras before it ever made it into battle.

CHARLES SUMNER

(1811-1874)

Boston-born Charles Sumner was a lawyer and a noted abolitionist before he was elected to the United States Senate on the Whig ticket in 1850. He strongly opposed the Kansas-Nebraska Act of 1854. In May 1856, in response to the border war that had broken out in Kansas, Sumner delivered his "Crime Against Kansas" speech, in which he denounced slavery and its supporters, some of them by name. Two days after he delivered the speech, Sumner was beaten unconscious by cane-wielding South Carolina Representative Preston S. Brooks. In 1857, Sumner joined the Republican Party. Although he campaigned for Abraham Lincoln in 1860, Sumner's beliefs regarding emancipation and civil rights for blacks diverged from the more moderate views of the president. The chair of the Senate Foreign Relations Committee as well as a leader of the Radical Republicans in the Senate, Sumner propounded his "Southern Suicide" theory in late 1862, which stated that, by seceding, the Confederate states had forfeited all of their rights under the United States Constitution. Sumner was one of the prime movers in President Andrew Johnson's impeachment in 1868. Later that year, President Ulysses S. Grant removed him from his Foreign Relations Committee position. Sumner devoted the last three years of his Senate career to working for the enactment of a sweeping Civil Rights Act that would guarantee fully integrated public accommodations. He died of a heart attack on May 11, 1874.

SURRENDER DATES

Contrary to popular belief, the Civil War did not end on April 9, 1865, when Confederate General Robert E. Lee surrendered to Union General Ulysses S. Grant at Appomattox Court House. Confederate General Joseph E. Johnston began discussing surrender terms with Union General William Tecumseh Sherman in North Carolina on April 17 and reached an accord on April 26, although his troops did not officially surrender until May 3. Confederate Lieutenant General Richard Taylor surrendered in Mobile, Alabama, to Union General E.R.S. Canby on May 4. Not realizing that Lee had surrendered, Confederate General E. Kirby Smith led his 350 men to a victory over Union General Theodore H. Barrett's force of more than 800 soldiers at Palmito Ranch in West Texas on May 12 and 13. Undaunted after learning of Lee's surrender, Smith went to Houston to raise more troops, but his subordinate, Lieutenant General Simon B. Buckner, surrendered in his name to Canby in New Orleans on May 26; Smith himself surrendered at Galveston, Texas, on June 2. Finally, on June 23, 1865, Confederate General Stand Watie surrendered to Union Lieutenant Colonel Asa C. Matthews at Doaksville, in the Indian Territory. The Civil War officially was over.

SURRENDER OF GEN. LEE!

"The Year of Jubilee has come! Let all the People Rejoice!"

200 GUNS WILL BE FIRED

On the Campus Martius,

AT 3 O'CLOCK TO-DAY, APRIL 10,

To Celebrate the Victories of our Armies.

Every Man, Woman and Child is hereby ordered to be on hand prepared to Sing and Rejoice. The crowd are expected to join in singing Patriotic Songs.

ALL PLACES OF BUSINESS MUST BE CLOSED AT 2 O'CLOCK.

Hurrah for Grant and his noble Army.

By Order of the People.

20 NEGRO ACT

In April 1862, the Confederate Congress passed the Conscription Bill. Because the draft was not well-received, the law was revised several times to change the age limits for military service and to amend the enumerated exemptions from service. The 20 Negro Act, passed in one of the revisions, exempted overseers and slaveowners who had 20 or more slaves; this was justified by the belief that a large contingent of slaves could be kept under control only by such an authority figure. Poor and non-slaveholding Confederate men saw this as favoring the rich. Conscription rules continued to be tightened until December 1863, when the Confederacy's desperate need for soldiers resulted in the elimination of virtually all exemptions.

TAXATION

Needing additional revenue to support the war effort, the Union government established a three percent income tax in 1861 for families earning more than $600 per year. The Internal Revenue Act of July 1862 authorized a more overarching system of taxation. The personal income tax rate was raised to five percent for annual incomes above $10,000. By 1864, the maximum tax rate was 10 percent. Additional taxes were levied on liquor, tobacco, medicine, luxury goods, professional licenses, and corporate income; the act also created stamp taxes, inheritance taxes, and value-added taxes. These new taxes raised almost $700 million, which financed more than 20 percent of the North's total war costs.

In April 1863, the Confederate Congress reluctantly enacted its own comprehensive tax program that included an income tax capped at one to two percent, profit, excise, and licensing taxes, and a controversial produce and livestock "tax in kind" that enabled the government to collect 10 percent of its farmers' output, which amounted to over $150 million worth of food. The inequities of in-kind taxation were addressed when the tax laws were revised in February 1864; farmers with holdings worth less than $500 were exempted, and wealthier farmers were taxed at a rate of five percent on the value of their land and slaves.

Although most of the federal taxes lapsed after the war, the income tax continued until 1872. An 1894 attempt to reinstitute a federal income tax was ruled unconstitutional by the Supreme Court. In February 1913, the ratification of the Sixteenth Amendment to the United States Constitution opened the way for the reestablishment of a federal income tax.

THIRTEENTH AMENDMENT

Almost three years after President Abraham Lincoln's Emancipation Proclamation had, on paper, freed all Confederate slaves, slavery was legally abolished in the United States when the Thirteenth Amendment was ratified in December 1865. First proposed in 1864, the amendment had failed to receive the necessary two-thirds majority vote in the Democrat-dominated House of Representatives. Interpreting his reelection as the people's endorsement of emancipation, Lincoln sought another vote; helped along by heavy lobbying and political favors, the amendment was passed on January 31, 1865.

A very different version of the amendment, which condoned slavery, had been contemplated by Congress in 1861 as a way to keep the Union together. Although it passed in both the House and Senate, the outbreak of the Civil War interrupted the ratification process and the proposed amendment died.

SALLY LOUISA TOMPKINS

(1833-1916)

The only female commissioned Confederate officer, Captain Sally Louisa Tompkins was a nurse who established the Robertson Hospital in Richmond on July 31, 1861, soon after the First Battle of Bull Run. She was commissioned by President Jefferson Davis to circumvent legislation that prohibited civilians from running military hospitals. During the course of the war, Tompkins supervised the care of more than 1,300 injured soldiers; only 73 of her patients died, an unusually low mortality rate for Civil-War-era hospitals. Tompkins closed the Robertson Hospital on June 13, 1865.

ROBERT AUGUSTUS TOOMBS

(1810-1885)

Robert Augustus Toombs, a lawyer and one of the richest planters in Georgia, began his political career in 1837, when he was elected to the Georgia legislature. Six years later, he went on to serve in the United States House of Representatives and, in 1853, the Senate. Toombs initially favored compromise to preserve the Union, but he became a secessionist after Lincoln was elected president. After resigning from the Senate in February 1861, he unsuccessfully sought the Confederate presidency. Instead, Toombs was appointed secretary of state. He resigned in July 1861 to undertake a more challenging role in the war, as a brigadier general in the Confederate army. General Toombs fought in the Seven Days campaign, the Second Battle of Bull Run, and, most notably, at Antietam. He left the military in July 1863, with a brief return in 1864 during Sherman's March to the Sea. In May 1865, Toombs went to Cuba and England to escape arrest. He returned to Georgia in 1867. Because of his refusal to apply for a pardon, he was prohibited from holding public office, although he remained active in Georgia politics. Robert Augustus Toombs died on December 15, 1885.

TRENT AFFAIR
(NOVEMBER-DECEMBER 1861)

In the fall of 1861, Confederate envoys James Mason and John Slidell were sent to Europe to enlist British and French support for the South. They left Charleston, South Carolina, on a blockade runner bound for Havana, where they boarded the *Trent*, a British mail steamer. Union Captain Charles Wilkes, the commander of the USS *San Jacinto*, fired on the *Trent* without orders and captured Mason and Slidell, who were taken to Fort Warren in Boston, Massachusetts. Although Wilkes briefly became a hero in the North, Britain protested this violation of its neutrality. Demanding an apology and the release of the prisoners, Britain sent troops to Canada, put its navy on war alert, and put an embargo on Indian saltpeter, a critical ingredient in gunpowder. War with Britain appeared to be imminent when Secretary of State William H. Seward convinced President Abraham Lincoln to release Mason and Slidell while continuing to assert the government's authority to have made the arrests. The two Confederates were released from prison on January 1, 1862, free to continue their ill-fated mission, and Britain was appeased.

SOJOURNER TRUTH
(1797(?)-1883)

Abolitionist and suffragist Sojourner Truth started life as a slave named Isabella Baumfree in Ulster County, New York. Treated cruelly and sold away from her family, she escaped in the 1820s and gained her freedom in 1828, when New York banned slavery. In 1843, after undergoing a religious experience, Baumfree changed her name to Sojourner Truth and began to speak out against slavery. Truth was a powerful orator whose vehement speeches brought the horrors of slavery vividly to life for her audiences as she traveled throughout New England and the Midwest. In 1864, President Abraham Lincoln invited her to the White House, in tribute to her efforts in support of African-American volunteer regiments. She was appointed to the National Freedman's Relief Association that same year and continued to work throughout her life to improve political and social conditions for black people. Sojourner Truth died in Battle Creek, Michigan, in 1883.

HARRIET TUBMAN

(1820(?)-1913)

Harriet Tubman was the most famous "conductor" on the Underground Railroad, as well as one of its beneficiaries. Born Araminta Ross, a slave, in Bucktown, Maryland, she adopted her mother's name, Harriet, as a child. When she was 13 years old, Harriet's skull was fractured by a two-pound iron weight as she tried to help another slave avoid punishment; as a result of her injury, she suffered from blackouts for the rest of her life. In 1844, Harriet Ross married John Tubman, a freed slave. Five years later, she left her husband behind and escaped to Philadelphia, Pennsylvania, where she worked as a maid and became an active abolitionist. Tubman responded to the Fugitive Slave Act of 1850 by joining the Underground Railroad, which had aided in her own escape. Making 18 or 19 clandestine trips to the South, she guided almost 300 slaves, including her sister and her parents, to freedom in the North. She never lost a slave, nor was she ever caught, although Confederate rewards for her capture peaked at approximately

$40,000. During the Civil War, she worked in South Carolina as a Union nurse, as a scout, and, occasionally, as a spy, and she participated in a military campaign that freed 756 slaves. Tubman returned to Auburn, New York, after the war and remained politically active, especially in the area of women's rights. In 1908, she established a home in Auburn for poor, elderly African-Americans. Harriet Tubman died on March 10, 1913. In the late 1850s, she had believed that John Brown, the radical abolitionist, would be the liberator of the slaves, but it is Harriet Tubman who is remembered as the "Moses" of her people.

UNCLE TOM'S CABIN

Uncle Tom's Cabin, Harriet Beecher Stowe's novel about slavery and the Old South, was serialized in the *National Era*, an abolitionist magazine, in 1851 and 1852. Published in book form in 1852, it became an immediate bestseller in the United States and in England. Soon after its publication, George L. Aiken turned the story into a play. This melodramatic version, and subsequent adaptations, came to represent *Uncle Tom's Cabin* in the popular culture, overshadowing the more balanced and realistic portrayal of slavery found in Stowe's novel. In Stowe's story, for example, Simon Legree, the brutal overseer, is a Northerner, and one of Tom's Southern owners debates the morality of slavery. Similarly, the novel characterizes Uncle Tom as a brave man who chooses to die rather than betray his friends; today, the term *Uncle Tom* has a negative, subservient connotation.

Stowe had hoped her novel would help to foster the process of emancipation. Instead, the various incarnations of *Uncle Tom's Cabin* galvanized the mutual antipathies of Northerners and Southerners and contributed to the growing sentiment for war.

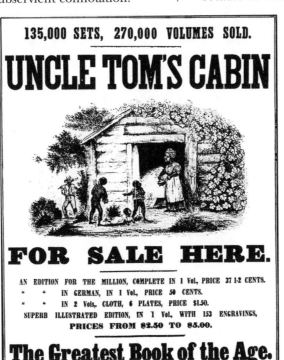

UNDERGROUND RAILROAD

During a 30-year period beginning around 1830, thousands of slaves escaped to freedom via the Underground Railroad, an informal network of African-American and white abolitionists who provided assistance in the form of food, clothing, money, and safe havens. Moving at night, and using whatever means of transportation they could find, fugitive slaves were guided northward by "conductors" and directed to hiding places, or "stations," in homes along their routes. The Underground Railroad had many "lines" running through Ohio, Indiana, and Western Pennsylvania; Philadelphia, with its large Quaker population, was also a major center. Because they risked capture in the Northern states, especially after the enactment of the Fugitive Slave Act of 1850, many runaways continued on to settle in Canada. Levi Coffin, a Quaker who lived in Indiana at the intersection of three major routes, was known as the "president" of the Underground Railroad because he assisted in the escapes of over 3,000 slaves.

Lucretia Mott and Susan B. Anthony, remembered for their activism on behalf of women's rights, also were active in the Underground Railroad. Although many free blacks and former slaves played important roles, the most famous African-American connected with the Underground Railroad was Harriet Tubman. Tubman used the system when she fled from her life as a slave and then made 18 or 19 more trips to the South, ultimately rescuing about 300 people.

Vallandigham (center) and his supporters.

CLEMENT LAIRD VALLANDIGHAM
(1820-1871)

Clement Laird Vallandigham was elected to the Ohio legislature in 1844. After several unsuccessful bids for Congress, he entered the United States House of Representatives in May 1858. A staunch advocate of states' rights and a vocal critic of President Abraham Lincoln, Vallandigham denounced the Civil War as unconstitutional. Redistricting cost the prominent Peace Democrat, or Copperhead, his House seat in 1862. Intentionally disregarding prohibitions on speech favorable to the Confederacy that had been imposed in April 1863 by Union General Ambrose B. Burnside, "Valiant Val" gave several speeches in which he referred to the invincibility of the South and called for the desertion of soldiers on both sides. Imprisoned by Burnside for treason, Lincoln ordered his release but exiled him to the Confederacy. His harsh criticisms of President

Confederate Libby Prison in Richmond, Virginia.

Jefferson Davis made Vallandigham equally unwelcome in the South, and he ran the blockade, escaping to Nassau and then to Canada. His Copperhead followers nominated him for governor of Ohio during his exile; he ran his campaign from southern Ontario but lost the election. Vallandigham returned to Ohio in June 1864. He delivered the keynote address at the Democratic convention that nominated General George B. McClellan for president and helped to formulate his peace platform. Vallandigham returned to his law practice after the war. He died on June 16, 1871, when his gun went off while he was demonstrating the manner in which a client might unintentionally have shot himself.

ELIZABETH VAN LEW
(1818-1900(?))

Richmond-born, Philadelphia-educated Elizabeth "Crazy Bet" Van Lew used her reputation as an eccentric to spy for the North. Her "humanitarian" visits to Libby Prison enabled some Union prisoners to escape. They also were a source of information, which she supplemented with reports from a former servant she had persuaded to infiltrate Jefferson Davis's home. Van Lew's coded messages were delivered directly to Union Generals Benjamin Butler and Ulysses S. Grant, secreted in baskets of farm produce. In recognition of her work for the Union, Grant named her postmistress of Richmond in 1869. After her term ended in 1877, she was supported by an annuity from the family of a Union soldier she had aided at Libby Prison.

LORETA JANETA VELAZQUEZ

(1842-?)

Born into the Spanish aristocracy in Cuba, Loreta Janeta Velazquez attended a convent school in New Orleans before eloping with a United States army officer in 1856 and moving to Fort Leavenworth. When the Civil War began and her husband enlisted in the Confederate army, she assumed a new identity, as Lieutenant Harry Buford, and organized a volunteer battalion. Velazquez served as her husband's aide-de-camp until his death, and then as a temporary company commander at the First Battle of Bull Run. Although her deception was uncovered in 1863, Velazquez, who had hoped to become the "second Joan of Arc," continued to work as a spy for the Confederacy. In 1876, Velazquez published a book about her exploits.

VETERAN RESERVE CORPS

Needing all of the soldiers it could find, the Union army established the Invalid Corps in 1863 for men who had been wounded or disabled in battle but who could undertake limited duty. Some members of the corps became guards in military prisons or at armories, while those who were more incapacitated served in army hospitals as nurses, orderlies, cooks, or clerks. Unfortunately, the initials of the corps also stood for "Inspected/Condemned," which was the code stamped on rejected army supplies; additionally, the uniforms issued to the Invalid Corps were light blue rather than the darker "Union blue" worn by the fighting troops. For these reasons, many wounded soldiers felt that they would be stigmatized if they joined the corps. In March 1864, to encourage greater participation, the Invalid Corps became the Veteran Reserve Corps and regulation army uniforms were issued to its members. By the time the war ended, at least 50,000 injured soldiers extended their military service by joining the corps. Some saw action, but most of them performed the mundane tasks needed to support the Union war effort.

VICKSBURG, CAMPAIGN AND SIEGE OF

(APRIL-JULY 4, 1863)

After a series of unsuccessful attempts to capture Vicksburg, Mississippi, Union General Ulysses S. Grant changed his strategy in April 1863. Instead of approaching the strategically critical city from its marshy northern side, his troops were transported across the Mississippi River under cover of darkness to prepare for a southern attack. To eliminate the possibility of reinforcement for Confederate General John C. Pemberton's defending forces, Grant turned his attention to Jackson, Mississippi, 45 miles to the east. On May 13, when Confederate General J. E. Johnston's 6,000 troops reached Jackson, it was too late. No match for the 25,000 Union soldiers awaiting them, the Confederates evacuated Jackson the next day. Grant then began a series of assaults on the Vicksburg, but the Confederate troops fought back tenaciously. By late May, Grant realized that he

would have to cut off the city and starve its defenders into submission. During the six-week Siege of Vicksburg, Union shelling went on day and night, depriving Confederate soldiers and civilians of rest and resulting in severe food shortages. On July 4, 1863, the day after the Union victory at Gettysburg, Pemberton agreed to Grant's terms of unconditional surrender; the remaining Southern stronghold, Port Hudson, Louisiana, surrendered on July 9. The Union now controlled the Mississippi River, effectively dividing the Confederacy in half and ensuring its demise.

WADE-DAVIS BILL
(JULY 1864)

The Radical Republicans in Congress not only contested President Abraham Lincoln's 1863 Proclamation of Amnesty and Reconstruction, but even his right as chief executive to set Reconstruction policy. Ohio Senator Benjamin F. Wade and Maryland Representative Henry Winter Davis sponsored a much harsher Reconstruction law that passed both houses of Congress in early July 1864. Under Lincoln's proclamation, a state could be readmitted to the Union if 10 percent of its white male citizens took a United States loyalty oath; acceptance of emancipation was implied.

The Wade-Davis Bill, however, required that 50 percent of a state's white male citizens had to take the oath, that a new state constitution explicitly guaranteeing emancipation must be adopted, and that Confederate officeholders and military volunteers were forever prohibited from government service. Lincoln's pocket veto of the law infuriated its sponsors, yet its practical effect was to defer Reconstruction plans until after the war, which was what the Radical Republicans had hoped to do.

MARY EDWARDS WALKER
(1832-1919)

Women's rights activist Mary Edwards Walker graduated in 1855 from Syracuse Medical College, where she was the only woman in her class. When the Civil War broke out, she volunteered for the Union army but was denied a commission as a surgeon. She worked as a nurse for almost three years before becoming the first woman to be commissioned as an army surgeon. Because she treated both Union and Confederate soldiers and civilians, she had free access between the lines and there is some speculation that she also worked as a spy. Walker was captured by the

Confederates and imprisoned for four months in 1864, until she was exchanged for a Confederate officer. After her release, she did not return to field duty, although she remained in the army until the end of the war. In 1865, Walker became the first woman to receive the Medal of Honor.

A "Bloomer Girl" who wore army uniforms during her military service and men's clothing afterwards, as well as a suffragist and a radical activist for equal rights for women, Walker founded "Adamless Eden," a women's separatist colony, in 1897. She received a military pension but had to supplement her income by appearing in carnival sideshows. Her Medal of Honor was among the 911 awards for non-combat duty, most from the Civil War-era, that were revoked when more restrictive eligibility criteria were enacted in 1916. She steadfastly refused to return her decoration, however, and continued to appeal the decision until she died, in 1919. Mary Edwards Walker's Medal of Honor ultimately was reinstated, but not until 1977, 58 years after her death.

WAR CORRESPONDENTS

Prior to the Civil War, newspaper stories often were nothing more than editorials, and national issues rarely were addressed. The advent of the war brought about a change to a more objective style of journalism. It also created new obstacles for reporters; military censorship of information about battles and troop movements led many journalists to resort to pseudonyms and subterfuge to get their stories into print. The Northern contingent of war correspondents grew to about 350 during the course of the war. Pooling their information and traveling in groups to follow the action, the reporters of the "Bohemian Brigade" made up the first American press corps.

In contrast to the burgeoning Northern press, many Southern newspapers went out of business as paper and other resources dwindled. Those that continued to publish lost their reporters to the

Confederate army and had to rely on reports from soldiers in the field and even on information obtained from Northern papers.

WAR DEMOCRATS

The Democratic Party was divided into two major factions during the Civil War. The Peace Democrats, or Copperheads, considered the war to be unconstitutional and supported the Confederacy. In contrast, the War Democrats wanted to restore the Union, were not necessarily opposed to slavery in the South, and generally supported President Abraham Lincoln. In the 1864 presidential election, the War Democrats combined with the Republican Party to form the Union Party, with Republican Lincoln and War Democrat Andrew Johnson as their candidates.

WASHINGTON, D.C.

When the Civil War began, Washington, D.C., was an unimpressive city of about 40,000 people. After a Confederate blockade of one approach to the city in the spring of 1861, however, the Union army began to build fortresses and batteries that ultimately would become a 37-mile ring of defenses surrounding the capital. As the war progressed, Washington experienced a major expansion, just as Richmond, the Confederate capital, did. By 1865, it had a population of 150,000. Along with new hospitals and prisons to handle an influx of wounded soldiers and prisoners, Washington's rapid growth made it a haven for speculators, entrepreneurs, and criminals. Unlike Richmond, however, the Union capital rarely lacked food or supplies. In 1864, Confederate General Jubal Early raided the outskirts of the city, but its defenses held strong and Washington remained firmly in Union control.

WASHINGTON PEACE CONFERENCE
(FEBRUARY 4-27, 1861)

In February 1861, a peace conference was held in Washington, D.C., in a final attempt to settle the slavery issue. The Washington Peace Conference, led by former President John Tyler, was attended by delegates from 21 states, with the greatest participation by the border states; the seven states that had already seceded did not participate, nor did Arkansas, California, Minnesota, Oregon, and Wisconsin. Congress rejected the delegates' recommendations for compromise.

STAND WATIE

(1806-1871)

General Stand Watie was the only Native American general in the Confederate army, and the highest-ranking Native American on either side. Before the war, the Georgia-born Cherokee was a planter and a journalist. He was active in the 1835 negotiations that resulted in the relocation of the Cherokee Nation from Georgia to the Indian Territory (Oklahoma); the three other Native Americans who signed the controversial agreement were murdered, but he escaped and became a tribal leader. Although the Cherokee Nation intended to remain neutral when the war broke out, the Confederacy promised them fairer treatment than they had received in the past and they allied themselves with the South in 1861. As commander of the Cherokee Mounted Rifles, Watie led his regiment in raids on Union supply lines in Missouri, Arkansas, and the Indian Territory, and was promoted to brigadier general in May 1864. Stand Watie was the last Confederate general to surrender, holding out until June 23, 1865. After the war, he returned to planting and tobacco manufacturing. He died in 1871.

WEST VIRGINIA

In the late spring of 1861, the western counties of Virginia, which had opposed secession, formed the Reorganized Government of Virginia in Wheeling. On June 20, 1863, the state of West Virginia was admitted to the Union.

The 6th Corps, Battle of the Wilderness, fighting in the woods

WILDERNESS, BATTLE OF THE
(MAY 5-6, 1864)

A year after the Confederate victory at the Battle of Chancellorsville, Union General Ulysses S. Grant and Confederate General Robert E. Lee fought for the first time. They met in "the Wilderness," the dense northern Virginia woods that still contained debris and human remains from Chancellorsville. When the fighting began on May 5, 1864, Union troops outnumbered Confederate troops 118,000 to 62,000, but the Confederates had the advantage of knowing the terrain. Visibility in the forest was so limited by the density of the trees as well as by the smoke from the battle and from the fires caused by the shelling, that the soldiers shot blindly and whole units could not find their way out. In two days of fighting, the North sustained 17,500 casualties to the South's 7,750; many of the dead had suffocated or been burned alive in the brushfires. Neither side could claim victory. Contrary to expectations, Grant did not retreat after the battle, but forged ahead toward Richmond and his next confrontation with Lee, at Spotsylvania Court House.

HENRY WIRZ
(1822-1865)

Confederate Captain Henry Wirz, the only person executed after the Civil War for war crimes, emigrated to the United States from Switzerland in 1849. He practiced medicine in Louisiana before enlisting in the Confederate army in 1861 and being assigned to a clerk position at Richmond's Libby Prison. Wirz was sent to

Europe as a purchasing agent after his right arm was permanently disabled when he was wounded at the Battle of Fair Oaks (Seven Pines) in May 1862. On his return in January 1864, he took command of Camp Sumter, better known as Andersonville Prison. Wirz made few, if any, attempts to improve the open-air camp's deplorable living conditions and even prohibited the building of shelters. Food and medical supplies were scarce, and most of the 12,912 Union soldiers who died at Andersonville succumbed to starvation, disease, and exposure. After the war, Wirz was convicted of "conspiracy to impair the health and destroy the lives of prisoners" by a military tribunal in Washington, D.C. He was hanged on November 10, 1865. Whether Wirz was guilty of intentional cruelty and murder or whether he was a scapegoat guilty only of being an ineffectual commander and a victim of the shortage of supplies that plagued the entire Confederacy is open to question.

"WOMAN ORDER"
(MAY 15, 1862)

As soon as New Orleans was occupied by Union forces in April 1862, Union General Benjamin Butler, the military governor of Louisiana, was confronted by many acts of resistance. These acts ranged from defiling the American flag to refusing to pledge allegiance to the Union. When the women of New Orleans began to express their contempt by taunting, spitting on, and otherwise abusing the occupying soldiers, Butler issued General Order No. 28, his infamous "Woman Order." Under the terms of this order, any woman who "by word, gesture, or movement" insulted a Union soldier would be arrested as a prostitute. Northerners and Southerners

were equally outraged by Butler's pronouncement, and even the Prime Minister of England spoke out against it. Although Butler achieved his goal, and few women were arrested, the controversial order was one of the factors that led to his being recalled from the military governorship on December 16, 1862.

WOMEN SOLDIERS IN THE CIVIL WAR

Although women served as nurses and in other supporting positions for both the North and the South during the Civil War, a number of women disguised themselves as men so that they could enlist as regular soldiers. Sarah Rosetta Wakeman, a.k.a. Private Lyons Wakeman, served for almost two years before her death in a military hospital in New Orleans. Sarah Emma Edmonds, who fought for the Union as Frank Thompson in the Second Michigan Infantry, chose to desert when she became ill with malaria and feared that her true identity would be revealed. Jennie Hodgers, an Irish stowaway, recreated herself as Albert D.J. Cashier, served with the Illinois Volunteer Infantry from 1862 until the war ended, and lived as a man for the rest of her life; her gender was discovered, but not betrayed, by a doctor at a veteran's hospital only after she was injured in an automobile accident in 1911, when she was 66 years old. Loreta Janeta Velasquez fought as Confederate Lieutenant Harry Buford until her masquerade was exposed, and then served as a spy.

Stories like these are not unique. In fact, historians believe that at least 400 women fought during the Civil War; approximately 60 women were injured or killed on the battlefield, and at least six soldiers revealed themselves to be female only when they gave birth during the war. These myriad deceptions were made possible because physical examinations at enlistment generally were perfunctory, young male enlistees often had high-pitched voices and no facial hair, and the social climate of the 1860s created the expectation that anyone who wore pants was a man.

FELIX KIRK ZOLLICOFFER (1812-1862)

Confederate General Felix Kirk Zollicoffer was the first general to die in the Civil War, under circumstances that came to be known as "Zollie's Folly." Born in Tennessee on May 19, 1812, Zollicoffer was a newspaper editor and fought in the Seminole War. As a Whig politician, he held several public offices and was a state legislator in Tennessee before serving in the United States House of Representatives from 1853 through 1859. Zollicoffer attended the Washington Peace Conference in 1861. As a brigadier general, he commanded forces in eastern Tennessee and southeastern Kentucky. In late 1861, his troops set up camp on the north side of the Cumberland River, not far from a Union encampment. The rainy weather and the proximity of the opposing forces made a river crossing too risky, and Zollicoffer was unwilling to attempt a move to the south side when ordered to do so by his commander, General G.B.

Crittenden. During a lull in the Battle of Logan Cross Roads (also known as Fishing Creek or Mill Springs) on January 19, 1862, Zollicoffer set out to do some reconnaissance, wearing a white raincoat that covered his uniform. He rode into the federal lines and told Union Colonel Speed S. Fry to cease firing on his own men. When Fry realized that this order came from a Confederate officer, he shot Zollicoffer in the chest, killing him.

ZOUAVES

Dressed in distinctive uniforms that typically included white canvas gaiters, baggy red pants, wide red or blue sashes, blue vests, and red capes, and a turban or a tasseled fez, Northern and Southern Zouave regiments stood out on Civil War battlefields. They patterned themselves after the Zouaves of the French colonial army, Algerian light infantry troops noted for their ability to fire and reload muskets while prone, as well as for their flamboyant uniforms. Union Colonel Elmer Ellsworth, the first officer killed in the war, organized the first American Zouave units.